M000103459

Holt McDougal Mathematics

Course 1
Know-It Notebook™

HOLT McDOUGAL
a division of Houghton Mifflin Harcourt

Copyright © Holt McDougal, a division of Houghton Mifflin Harcourt Publishing Company. All rights reserved.

Warning: No part of this work may be reproduced or transmitted in any form or by any means, electronic or mechanical, including photocopying and recording, or by any information storage or retrieval system without the prior written permission of Holt McDougal unless such copying is expressly permitted by federal copyright law.

Requests for permission to make copies of any part of the work should be mailed to the following address: Permissions Department, Holt McDougal, 10801 N. MoPac Expressway, Building 3, Austin, Texas 78759.

HOLT McDOUGAL is a trademark of Houghton Mifflin Harcourt Publishing Company.

Printed in the United States of America

If you have received these materials as examination copies free of charge, Holt McDougal retains title to the materials and they may not be resold. Resale of examination copies is strictly prohibited.

Possession of this publication in print format does not entitle users to convert this publication, or any portion of it, into electronic format.

ISBN 13: 978-0-55-400516-4
ISBN 10: 0-55-400516-6

1 2 3 4 5   073   12 11 10 09 08

Contents

Introduction

Using the Know-It Notebook™ v

Note Taking Strategies vii

Chapter 1

Lesson 1-1 1

Lesson 1-2 4

Lesson 1-3 7

Lesson 1-4 10

Lesson 1-5 12

Lesson 1-6 13

Chapter Review 15

Big Ideas 17

Chapter 2

Lesson 2-1 18

Lesson 2-2 20

Lesson 2-3 22

Lesson 2-4 24

Lesson 2-5 26

Lesson 2-6 28

Lesson 2-7 30

Lesson 2-8 33

Chapter Review 35

Big Ideas 38

Chapter 3

Lesson 3-1 39

Lesson 3-2 41

Lesson 3-3 45

Lesson 3-4 48

Lesson 3-5 50

Lesson 3-6 53

Lesson 3-7 55

Lesson 3-8 58

Lesson 3-9 60

Chapter Review 63

Big Ideas 66

Chapter 4

Lesson 4-1 67

Lesson 4-2 69

Lesson 4-3 71

Lesson 4-4 74

Lesson 4-5 77

Lesson 4-6 79

Lesson 4-7 81

Lesson 4-8 84

Lesson 4-9 86

Chapter Review 88

Big Ideas 92

Chapter 5

Lesson 5-1 93

Lesson 5-2 96

Lesson 5-3 99

Lesson 5-4 101

Lesson 5-5 103

Lesson 5-6 105

Lesson 5-7 108

Lesson 5-8 110

Lesson 5-9 112

Lesson 5-10 114

Chapter Review 116

Big Ideas 120

Chapter 6

Lesson 6-1 121

Lesson 6-2 123

Lesson 6-3 126

Lesson 6-4 129

Lesson 6-5 133

Lesson 6-6 136

Lesson 6-7 138

Lesson 6-8 141

Lesson 6-9 144

Lesson 6-10 146

Chapter Review 148

Big Ideas 152

Copyright © by Holt McDougal.
All rights reserved.

Holt McDougal Mathematics

Contents

Chapter 7

Lesson 7-1 153
Lesson 7-2 156
Lesson 7-3 158
Lesson 7-4 161
Lesson 7-5 164
Lesson 7-6 166
Lesson 7-7 168
Lesson 7-8 171
Lesson 7-9 173
Lesson 7-10 175
Chapter Review 178
Big Ideas .181

Chapter 8

Lesson 8-1 182
Lesson 8-2 184
Lesson 8-3 187
Lesson 8-4 189
Lesson 8-5 191
Lesson 8-6 194
Lesson 8-7 196
Lesson 8-8 199
Lesson 8-9 202
Lesson 8-10 204
Lesson 8-11 206
Chapter Review 209
Big Ideas .213

Chapter 9

Lesson 9-1 214
Lesson 9-2 216
Lesson 9-3 218
Lesson 9-4 220
Lesson 9-5 222
Lesson 9-6 224
Lesson 9-7 227
Lesson 9-8 230
Chapter Review 233
Big Ideas .236

Chapter 10

Lesson 10-1 237
Lesson 10-2 239
Lesson 10-3 241
Lesson 10-4 243
Lesson 10-5 245
Lesson 10-6 247
Lesson 10-7 249
Lesson 10-8 251
Lesson 10-9 253
Chapter Review 256
Big Ideas .259

Chapter 11

Lesson 11-1 260
Lesson 11-2 262
Lesson 11-3 264
Lesson 11-4 266
Lesson 11-5 268
Lesson 11-6 270
Lesson 11-7 271
Lesson 11-8 272
Lesson 11-9 273
Chapter Review 274
Big Ideas .277

Chapter 12

Lesson 12-1 278
Lesson 12-2 280
Lesson 12-3 282
Lesson 12-4 285
Lesson 12-5 287
Lesson 12-6 289
Chapter Review 292
Big Ideas .295

Chapter 13

Lesson 13-1 296
Lesson 13-2 299
Lesson 13-3 302
Lesson 13-4 304
Lesson 13-5 306
Lesson 13-6 308
Chapter Review 310
Big Ideas .312

Copyright © by Holt McDougal.
All rights reserved.

Holt McDougal Mathematics

Introduction

Using the Know-It Notebook™

This *Know-It Notebook* will help you take notes, organize your thinking, and study for quizzes and tests. There are *Know-It Notes*™ pages for every lesson in your textbook. These notes will help you identify important mathematical information that you will need later.

Know-It Notes

Lesson Objectives

A good note-taking practice is to know the objective the content covers.

Vocabulary

Another good note-taking practice is to keep a list of the new vocabulary.

- Use the page references or the glossary in your textbook to find each definition.
- Write each definition on the lines provided.

Additional Examples

Your textbook includes examples for each math concept taught. Additional examples in the *Know-It Notebook* help you take notes so you remember how to solve different types of problems.

- Take notes as your teacher discusses each example.
- Write notes in the blank boxes to help you remember key concepts.
- Write final answers in the shaded boxes.

Check It Out!

Complete the Check It Out! problems that follow some lessons. Use these to make sure you understand the math concepts covered in the lesson.

- Write each answer in the space provided.
- Check your answers with your teacher or another student.
- Ask your teacher to help you understand any problem that you answered incorrectly.

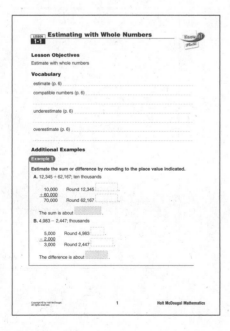

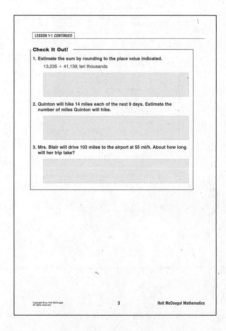

Copyright © by Holt McDougal.
All rights reserved.

Holt McDougal Mathematics

Introduction

Chapter Review

Complete Chapter Review problems that follow each chapter. This is a good review before you take the chapter test.

- Write each answer in the space provided.
- Check your answers with your teacher or another student.
- Ask your teacher to help you understand any problem that you answered incorrectly.

Big Ideas

The Big Ideas have you summarize the important chapter concepts in your own words. You must think about and understand ideas to put them in your own words. This will also help you remember them.

- Write each answer in the space provided.
- Check your answers with your teacher or another student.
- Ask your teacher to help you understand any question that you answered incorrectly.

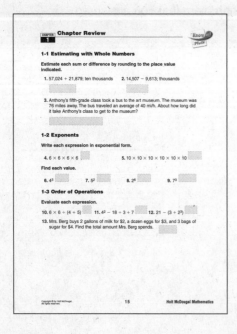

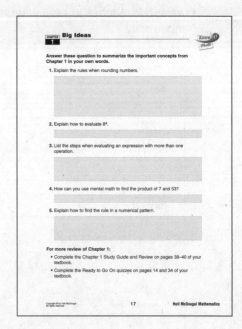

Copyright © by Holt McDougal.
All rights reserved.

Holt McDougal Mathematics

Introduction

Note Taking Strategies

Taking good notes is very important in many of your classes and will be even more important when you take college classes. This notebook was designed to help you get started. Here are some other steps that can help you take good notes.

Getting Ready

1. Use a loose-leaf notebook. You can add pages to this where and when you want to. It will help keep you organized.

During the Lecture

2. If you are taking notes during a lecture, write the big ideas. Use abbreviations to save time. Do not worry about spelling or writing every word. Use headings to show changes in the topics discussed. Use numbering or bullets to organize supporting ideas under each topic heading. Leave space before each new heading so that you can fill in more information later.

After the Lecture

3. As soon as possible after the lecture, read through your notes and add any information that will help you understand them when you review later. You should also summarize the information into key words or key phrases. This will help your comprehension and will help you process the information. These key words and key phrases will be your memory cues when you are reviewing for or taking a test. At this time you may also want to write questions to help clarify the meaning of the ideas and facts.

4. Read your notes out loud. As you do this, state the ideas in your own words and do as much as you can by memory. This will help you remember and will also help with your thinking process. This activity will help you understand the information.

5. Reflect upon the information you have learned. Ask yourself how new information relates to information you already know. Ask how this relates to your personal experience. Ask how you can apply this information and why it is important.

Before the Test

6. Review your notes. Don't wait until the night before the test to review. Do frequent reviews. Don't just read through your notes. Put the information in your notes into your own words. If you do this you will be able to connect the new material with material you already know, and you will be better prepared for tests. You will have less test anxiety and better recall.

7. Summarize your notes. This should be in your own words and should only include the main points you need to remember. This will help you internalize the information.

Copyright © by Holt McDougal.
All rights reserved.

Holt McDougal Mathematics

Estimating with Whole Numbers

Lesson Objectives

Estimate with whole numbers

Vocabulary

estimate (p. 6) _____

compatible numbers (p. 6) _____

_____

underestimate (p. 6) _____

_____

overestimate (p. 6) _____

Additional Examples

Example 1

Estimate the sum or difference by rounding to the place value indicated.

A. 12,345 + 62,167; ten thousands

$$
\begin{array}{r}
10,000 \\
+\,60,000 \\
\hline
70,000
\end{array}
$$
Round 12,345 ☐.

Round 62,167 ☐.

The sum is about ☐.

B. 4,983 − 2,447; thousands

$$
\begin{array}{r}
5,000 \\
-\,2,000 \\
\hline
3,000
\end{array}
$$
Round 4,983 ☐.

Round 2,447 ☐.

The difference is about ☐.

Copyright © by Holt McDougal.
All rights reserved.

Holt McDougal Mathematics

Example 2

Chelsea is planning the annual softball banquet for the 8 teams in the region. Each team has 18 members. Estimate how many plates she will need to buy if all the members attend.

$$8 \times 18 \longrightarrow 8 \times 20$$

$$8 \times 20 = 160$$

[   ] the number of team members.

The actual number of team members is [   ] than 160.

If Chelsea buys [   ] plates, she will have enough for each person.

Example 3

Mr. Dehmel will drive 243 miles to the fair at 65 mi/h. About how long will his trip take?

$$243 \div 65 \longrightarrow 240 \div 60$$

$$240 \div 60 = 4$$

240 and 60 are [   ] numbers. Underestimate

the speed.

Because he underestimated the speed, the actual time will be

[   ] hours.

Copyright © by Holt McDougal.
All rights reserved.

Holt McDougal Mathematics

Check It Out!

1. **Estimate the sum by rounding to the place value indicated.**

   13,235 + 41,139; ten thousands

2. **Quinton will hike 14 miles each of the next 9 days. Estimate the number of miles Quinton will hike.**

3. **Mrs. Blair will drive 103 miles to the airport at 55 mi/h. About how long will her trip take?**

Copyright © by Holt McDougal.
All rights reserved.

Holt McDougal Mathematics

Exponents

Lesson Objectives

Represent numbers by using exponents

Vocabulary

exponent (p. 10) _____

_____

base (p. 10) _____

_____

exponential form (p. 10) _____

_____

Additional Examples

Example 1

Write each expression in exponential form.

A. $5 \times 5 \times 5 \times 5$

[ ]   5 is a factor 4 times.

B. $3 \times 3 \times 3 \times 3 \times 3$

[ ]   [ ] is a factor [ ] times.

Example 2

Find each value.

A. 2^6

$2^6 = 2 \times 2 \times 2 \times 2 \times 2 \times 2 = $ [ ]

B. 4^5

$4^5 = $ [ ] $ = $ [ ]

Copyright © by Holt McDougal.
All rights reserved.

Holt McDougal Mathematics

Example 3   PROBLEM SOLVING APPLICATION

A phone tree is used to contact families at Paul's school. The secretary calls 4 families. Then each family calls 4 other families, and so on. How many families will be notified during the fourth round of calls?

1. **Understand the Problem**
   The answer will be the number of families called in the 4th round. List the important information:

   - The secretary calls ☐ families.

   - Each family calls ☐ families.

2. **Make a Plan**
   You can draw a diagram to see how many calls are in each round.

   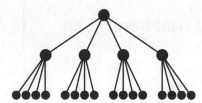

   Secretary

   1st round — ☐ calls

   2nd round — ☐ calls

3. **Solve**
   Notice that in each round, the number of calls is a power of 4.

   1st round: 4 calls $= 4 = 4^1$

   2nd round: 16 calls $=$ ☐ $= 4^2$

   So during the fourth round, there will be 4^4 calls.

   $4^4 =$ ☐ $=$ ☐

   During the 4th round of calls, ☐ families will be notified.

4. **Look Back**
   Drawing a diagram helps you see how to use exponents to solve the problem.

Copyright © by Holt McDougal.
All rights reserved.

5

Holt McDougal Mathematics

Check It Out!

1. Write the expression in exponential form.

$$6 \times 6 \times 6 \times 6 \times 6 \times 6 = \boxed{}$$

2. Find the value.

$$3^4 = \boxed{}$$

3. Problem Solving Application
A phone tree is used to contact families at Emily's work. The secretary calls 3 employees. Then each employee calls 3 other employees, and so on. How many employees will be notified during the fourth round of calls?

1. Understand the Problem
The answer will be the number of employees called in the fourth round.

List the important information:

- The secretary calls $\boxed{}$ employees.

- Each employee calls $\boxed{}$ employees.

2. Make a Plan

3. Solve

4. Look Back
Drawing a diagram helps you see how to use exponents to solve the problem.

Copyright © by Holt McDougal.
All rights reserved.

Holt McDougal Mathematics

Order of Operations

Lesson Objectives

Use the order of operations

Vocabulary

numerical expression (p. 18) _____

_____

simplify (p. 18) _____

_____

order of operations (p. 18) _____

_____

_____

Simplify Examples

Example 1

Simplify each expression.

A. $15 - 10 \div 2$ There are no parentheses or exponents.

$15 - \boxed{}$ Divide.

$\boxed{}$ Subtract.

B. $9 + (21 \div 7) \times 5$

$9 + \boxed{} \times 5$ Perform operations within $\boxed{}$.

$9 + \boxed{}$ $\boxed{}$.

$\boxed{}$ Add.

Example 2

Simplify each expression.

A. $2^4 + 6 \times 4$

$\boxed{} + 6 \times 4$ Find the value of numbers with $\boxed{}$.

$16 + \boxed{}$ $\boxed{}$.

$\boxed{}$ Add.

B. $24 \div (9 - 6) \times 3^2 - 10$

$24 \div \boxed{} \times 3^2 - 10$ Perform operations within $\boxed{}$.

$24 \div 3 \times \boxed{} - 10$ Find the value of numbers with $\boxed{}$.

$\boxed{} \times 9 - 10$ $\boxed{}$.

$\boxed{} - 10$ $\boxed{}$.

$\boxed{}$ Subtract.

Example 3

Mr. Kellett bought 6 used CDs for $4 each and 5 used CDs for $3 each. Simplify the following expression to find the amount Mr. Kellett spent on CDs.

$$6 \times 4 + 5 \times 3$$

$$\boxed{} + \boxed{}$$

$$\boxed{}$$

Mr. Kellett spent $\boxed{}$ on CDs.

Copyright © by Holt McDougal.
All rights reserved.

Holt McDougal Mathematics

Check It Out!

1. Simplify the expression.

   $2 \times (3 + 6) + 4$

2. Simplify $16 + 5^2 \times 3$.

3. Ms. Nivia bought 4 new CDs for $8 each and 6 used CDs for $4 each. Simplify the following expression to find the amount Ms. Nivia spent on CDs.

   $4 \times 8 + 6 \times 4$

Copyright © by Holt McDougal.
All rights reserved.

Holt McDougal Mathematics

Properties and Mental Math

Lesson Objectives

Use number properties to compute mentally

Vocabulary

Commutative Property (p. 22) _____

_____

_____

Associative Property (p. 22) _____

_____

_____

Distributive Property (p. 23) _____

_____

_____

Additional Examples

Example 1

A. Simplify 17 + 5 + 3 + 15.

17 + 5 + 3 + 15	Look for sums that are multiples of [ ].
17 + 3 + 5 + 15	Use the [ ] Property.
(17 + 3) + (5 + 15)	Use the [ ] Property to
[ ] + [ ]	make groups of [ ]
[ ]	numbers. Use [ ] math to add.

Copyright © by Holt McDougal.
All rights reserved.

Holt McDougal Mathematics

B. Simplify 4 × 13 × 5.

13 × 4 × 5   Use the [   ] Property.

13 × (4 × 5)   Use the [   ] Property to

13 × [   ]   group [   ] numbers.

[   ]   Use [   ] math to multiply.

Example 2

Use the Distributive Property to find each product.

A. 6 × 35

6 × 35 = 6 × (30 + 5)   "Break apart" 35 into [   ] + [   ].

= (6 × 30) + (6 × 5)   [   ] Property

= [   ] + [   ]   Use [   ] math to multiply.

= [   ]   Use [   ] math to [   ].

B. 9 × 87

9 × 87 = 9 × ([   ] + [   ])   "Break apart" 87 into [   ] + [   ].

= (9 × [   ]) + (9 × [   ])   [   ] Property.

= [   ] + [   ]   Use [   ] math to multiply.

= [   ]   Use [   ] math to [   ].

Check It Out!

1. Simplify 12 + 5 + 8 + 5.   **2. Simplify 6 × 43.**

[   ]   [   ]

Copyright © by Holt McDougal.
All rights reserved.

Holt McDougal Mathematics

Choosing a Method of Computation

Lesson Objectives

Choose an appropriate method of computation and justify a choice

Additional Examples

Example 1

A. Simplify the expression and state the method of computation you used.

$4 + 3 + 2 + 10 + 8 + 2 + 5 + 1$

There are probably too many numbers to add [_____], but the

numbers are small. You can use paper and pencil. [____]

B. 4,562 − 397

397 is close to a multiple of [____].

You can use mental math.

$(4,562 + 3) − (397 + 3)$ Think: Add 3 to 397 to make [____].

[____] − [____]   Add 3 to [_____] to compensate.

[_____]

Check It Out!

1. Find the difference: 3,442 − 298.

Copyright © by Holt McDougal.
All rights reserved.

Holt McDougal Mathematics

Patterns and Sequences

Lesson Objectives

Find, recognize, describe, and extend patterns in sequences

Vocabulary

sequence (p. 29) _____

_____

term (p. 29) _____

_____

arithmetic sequence (p. 29) _____

Additional Examples

Example 1

Identify a pattern in each sequence and then find the missing terms.

A. 48, 42, 36, 30, □, □, □, . . .

A pattern is to subtract ☐ from each term to get the next term.

30 − 6 = ☐   24 − 6 = ☐   18 − 6 = ☐

So ☐, ☐, and ☐ will be the next three terms.

B.

Position	1	2	3	4	5	6
Value of Term	9	22	35	48	□	□

A pattern is to add ☐ to each term.

48 + 13 = ☐   61 + 13 = ☐

So ☐ and ☐ will be the next terms.

Copyright © by Holt McDougal.
All rights reserved.

Holt McDougal Mathematics

Example 2

Identify a pattern in each sequence. Name the missing terms.

A. 24, 34, 31, 41, 38, 48, ☐, ☐, ☐, . . .

One pattern is to add ☐ to one term and subtract ☐ from the next.

48 − 3 = ☐   45 + 10 = ☐   55 − 3 = ☐

So ☐, ☐, and ☐ will be the next three terms.

B.

Position	1	2	3	4	5	6	7
Value of Term	1	4	2	8	☐	16	☐

A pattern is to ☐ one term by ☐ and divide the next term

by ☐.

8 ÷ 2 = ☐   16 ÷ 2 = ☐

So ☐ and ☐ are the missing terms.

Check It Out!

1. Identify a pattern in the sequence. Name the next three terms.

12, 23, 34, ☐, ☐, ☐, . . .

2. Identify a pattern in the sequence. Name the missing terms.

8, 2, 16, 4, 32, ☐, 64, 16, ☐, . . .

Copyright © by Holt McDougal.
All rights reserved.

Holt McDougal Mathematics

1-1 Estimating with Whole Numbers

Estimate each sum or difference by rounding to the place value indicated.

1. 57,024 + 21,879; ten thousands

2. 14,507 − 9,613; thousands

3. Anthony's fifth-grade class took a bus to the art museum. The museum was 76 miles away. The bus traveled an average of 40 mi/h. About how long did it take Anthony's class to get to the museum?

1-2 Exponents

Write each expression in exponential form.

4. $6 \times 6 \times 6 \times 6$

5. $10 \times 10 \times 10 \times 10 \times 10 \times 10$

Find each value.

6. 4^3 **7.** 5^2 **8.** 2^6 **9.** 7^3

1-3 Order of Operations

Evaluate each expression.

10. $6 \times 6 \div (4 + 5)$ **11.** $4^2 − 18 \div 3 + 7$ **12.** $21 − (3 + 2^3)$

13. Mrs. Berg buys 2 gallons of milk for $2, a dozen eggs for $3, and 3 bags of sugar for $4. Find the total amount Mrs. Berg spends.

Copyright © by Holt McDougal.
All rights reserved.

Holt McDougal Mathematics

1-4 Properties and Mental Math

Use mental math to find each sum or product.

14. $23 + 12 + 7 + 18$ ⬜

15. $2 \times 13 \times 5$ ⬜

Use the Distributive Property to find each product.

16. 2×56 ⬜

17. 8×36 ⬜

18. The temperature on Monday was 63°F. The temperature was predicted to drop 4°F on Tuesday, rise 7°F on Wednesday, rise 2°F on Thursday, and drop 5°F on Friday. What was the predicted temperature on Friday? ⬜

1-5 Choosing a Method of Computation

Choose a solution method and solve. Explain your choice.

19. Jamie receives $7.25 a week as allowance. How much does she receive in four weeks? ⬜

20. A factory produces 238 baseballs per minute. How many baseballs are produced in 360 minutes? ⬜

1-6 Patterns and Sequences

Use the pattern below to write the first five terms of the sequence.

21. Start with 7, add 2. ⬜

22. Start with 3, multiply by 5. ⬜

Copyright © by Holt McDougal.
All rights reserved.

Holt McDougal Mathematics

Big Ideas

Answer these question to summarize the important concepts from Chapter 1 in your own words.

1. Explain the rules when rounding numbers.

2. Explain how to evaluate 8^4.

3. List the steps when evaluating an expression with more than one operation.

4. How can you use mental math to find the product of 7 and 53?

5. Explain how to find the rule in a numerical pattern.

For more review of Chapter 1:

- Complete the Chapter 1 Study Guide and Review on pages 38–40 of your textbook.

- Complete the Ready to Go On quizzes on pages 14 and 34 of your textbook.

Copyright © by Holt McDougal.
All rights reserved.

Holt McDougal Mathematics

Variables and Expressions

Lesson Objectives

Identify and evaluate expressions

Vocabulary

variable (p. 50) _____

_____

constant (p. 50) _____

_____

algebraic expression (p. 50) _____

_____

evaluate (p. 50) _____

_____

Additional Examples

Example 1

Evaluate each expression to find the missing values in the table.

A.

y	$5 \times y$
16	80
27	
35	

Substitute for y in $5 \times y$.

$y = 16; 5 \times 16 = 80$

$y = 27; 5 \times 27 = \boxed{}$

$y = \boxed{}; 5 \times \boxed{} = \boxed{}$

B.

z	$z \div 5 + 4$
20	8
45	
60	

Substitute for z in $z \div 5 + 4$.

$z = 20; 20 \div 5 + 4 = 8$

$z = 45; \boxed{} \div 5 + 4 = \boxed{}$

$z = \boxed{}; \boxed{} \div 5 + 4 = \boxed{}$

Copyright © by Holt McDougal.
All rights reserved.

Holt McDougal Mathematics

Example 2

A rectangle is 4 units wide. What is the area of the rectangle if it is 3, 4, 5, or 6 units long?

l	w	l × w
3	4	12
4	4	
5	4	
6	4	

Make a [   ] to help you find the number of square units for each length.

$3 \times 4 = 12$ square units

$4 \times 4 =$ [   ] square units

$5 \times 4 =$ [   ] square units

$6 \times 4 =$ [   ] square units

Check It Out!

1. Complete the table.

z	8 × z + 2
7	58
9	
11	

2. A rectangle is 7 units wide. What is the area of the rectangle if it is 8, 9, 10, or 11 units long?

Copyright © by Holt McDougal.
All rights reserved.

19

Holt McDougal Mathematics

Translating Between Words and Math

Lesson Objectives

Translate between words and math

Additional Examples

Example 1

A. Lake Superior is the largest lake in North America. Let *a* stand for the area in square miles of Lake Superior. Lake Erie has an area of 9,910 square miles. Write an expression to show how much larger Lake Superior is than Lake Erie.

To find how much larger, subtract the area of Lake Erie from the area of Lake Superior.

$$a - \boxed{}$$

Lake Superior is $\boxed{}$ square miles larger than Lake Erie.

B. Let *p* represent the number of colored pencils in a box. If there are 26 boxes on the shelf, write an algebraic expression to represent the total number of pencils on the shelf.

To put together 26 equal groups of *p*, multiply $\boxed{}$ times *p*.

$$\boxed{} \, p$$

There are $\boxed{}$ pencils on the shelf.

Example 2

Write each phrase as a numerical or algebraic expression.

A. 987 minus 12

987 $\boxed{}$ 12

B. *x* times 45

45 $\boxed{}$ *x* or $\boxed{}$

Copyright © by Holt McDougal.
All rights reserved.

Holt McDougal Mathematics

Example 3

Write two phrases for each expression.

A. $\dfrac{16}{b}$

     • 16 [ ] *b*

     • the [ ] of 16 and *b*

B. $(75)(32)$

     • 75 [ ] 32

     • the [ ] of 75 and 32

Check It out!

1. The Nile River is the world's longest river. Let *n* stand for the length in miles of the Nile. The Paraná River is 3,030 miles long. Write an expression to show how much longer the Nile is than the Paraná.

2. Write the phrase as a numerical or algebraic expression.

   42 more than 79

3. Write two phrases for the expression.

   $18 - r$

Copyright © by Holt McDougal.
All rights reserved.

Holt McDougal Mathematics

Translating Between Tables and Expressions

Lesson Objectives

Write expressions for tables and sequences

Example 1

Write an expression for the missing value in the table.

Spike's Age	Rusty's Age
2	6
3	7
4	8
a	

Rusty's age is Spike's age plus ⬚.

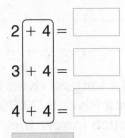

$2 + 4 = $ ⬚

$3 + 4 = $ ⬚

$4 + 4 = $ ⬚

Example 2

Write an expression for the sequence in the table.

Position	1	2	3	4	n
Value	7	10	13	16	

Look for a relationship between the ⬚ and the

⬚ of the terms in the sequence. Use guess and check.

Guess $7n$
Check by substituting 2.

⬚ $\cdot 2$ does not equal 10.

Guess $3n + 2$.
Check by substituting 2.

⬚ $\cdot 2 + $ ⬚ does not equal 10.

Guess $3n + 4$.
Check by substituting 2.

⬚ $\cdot 2 + $ ⬚ $= $ ⬚

The expression ⬚ works for the entire sequence.

$3 \cdot 1 + 4 = $ ⬚ , $3 \cdot 2 + 4 = $ ⬚ , $3 \cdot 3 + 4 = $ ⬚ , $3 \cdot 4 + 4 = $ ⬚

Copyright © by Holt McDougal.
All rights reserved.

Holt McDougal Mathematics

Example 3

A triangle has a base of 6 inches. The table shows the area of the triangle for different heights. Write an expression that can be used to find the area of the triangle when its height is *h* inches.

Base (in.)	Height (in.)	Area (in²)
6	1	3
6	2	6
6	4	12
6	*h*	

$6 \times 1 = 6, 6 \div 2 = 3$

$6 \times 2 = \boxed{}, 12 \div 2 = \boxed{}$

$6 \times 4 = \boxed{}, 24 \div 2 = \boxed{}$

$6 \times h = \boxed{}, 6h \div 2 = 3h$

Check It Out!

1. Write an expression for the missing value in the table.

Trucks	2	3	4	*t*
Tires	12	18	24	

2. Write an expression for the sequence in the table.

Position	1	2	3	4	*n*
Value	7	9	11	13	

3. A triangle has a base of 10 inches. The table shows the area of the triangle for different heights. Write an expression that can be used to find the area of the triangle when its height is *h* inches.

Height (in.)	1	2	4	*h*
Area (in²)	5	10	20	

Equations and Their Solutions

Lesson Objectives

Determine whether a number is a solution of an equation

Vocabulary

equation (p. 66) _____

_____

solution (p. 66) _____

_____

Additional Examples

Example 1

Determine whether the given value of each variable is a solution.

A. $b - 447 = 1,203$ for $b = 1,650$

$$b - 447 = 1,203$$

$1,650 - 447 \overset{?}{=} 1,203$ [_____] 1,650 for b.

$1,203 \overset{?}{=} 1,203$ [_____].

Because [_____] = [_____],

1,650 is a solution to $b - 447 = 1,203$.

B. $27x = 1,485$ for $x = 54$

$$27x = 1,485$$

$27 \cdot 54 \overset{?}{=} 1,485$ [_____] 54 for x.

$1,458 \overset{?}{=} 1,485$ [_____].

Because [_____] ≠ [_____],

54 is not a solution to $27x = 1,485$.

Example 2

Paulo says that the park is 19 yards long. Jamie says that the park is 664 inches long. Determine if these two measurements are equal.

$36 \cdot y = i$

$36 \cdot y = 664$

$36 \cdot 19 \overset{?}{=} 664$ Substitute ☐ for y.

$684 \overset{?}{=} 664$ ☐.

Because ☐ $\neq$ ☐ , 19 yards is not equal to 664 inches.

Check It Out!

1. Determine whether the given value of the variable is a solution.

$u + 56 = 139$ for $u = 73$

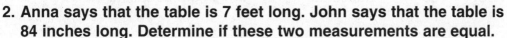

2. Anna says that the table is 7 feet long. John says that the table is 84 inches long. Determine if these two measurements are equal.

Copyright © by Holt McDougal.
All rights reserved.

Holt McDougal Mathematics

Addition Equations

Lesson Objectives

Solve whole-number addition equations

Vocabulary

Inverse operations (p. 70) _____

Additional Examples

Example 1

Solve each equation. Check your answers.

A. $x + 87 = 152$

| $x + 87 =$ | 152 | 87 is added to x. |

| $-\ 87$ | $-\ 87$ | [ ] 87 from both sides to |

undo the [ ].

x $=$ [ ]

Check $x + 87 = 152$

$65 + 87 \stackrel{?}{=} 152$ Substitute [ ] for x in the equation.

$152 \stackrel{?}{=} 152 \checkmark$ [ ] is the solution.

B. $72 = 18 + y$

| $72 =$ | $18 + y$ | 18 is added to y. |

| $-\ 18$ | $-\ 18$ | [ ] 18 from both sides to |

undo the [ ].

[ ] $=$ y

Check $72 = 18 + y$

$72 \stackrel{?}{=} 18 + 54$ Substitute [ ] for y in the equation.

$72 \stackrel{?}{=} 72 \checkmark$ [ ] is the solution.

Copyright © by Holt McDougal.
All rights reserved.

Holt McDougal Mathematics

Example 2

Johnstown, Cooperstown, and Springfield are located in that order in a straight line along a highway. It is 12 miles from Johnstown to Cooperstown and 95 miles from Johnstown to Springfield. Find the distance *d* between Cooperstown and Springfield.

distance between Johnstown and Springfield	=	distance between Johnstown and Cooperstown	+	distance between Cooperstown and Springfield
95	=	12	+	*d*

$95 = 12 + d$ 12 is added to *d*.

$-12 \quad -12$ [   ] 12 from both sides to undo

the [   ].

[   ] $= d$

It is [   ] miles from Cooperstown to Springfield.

Check It Out!

1. Solve the equation. Check your answer.

$u + 43 = 78$

2. Patterson, Jacobsville, and East Valley are located in that order in a straight line along a highway. It is 17 miles from Patterson to Jacobsville and 35 miles from Patterson to East Valley. Find the distance *d* between Jacobsville and East Valley.

Copyright © by Holt McDougal.
All rights reserved.

Holt McDougal Mathematics

Subtraction Equations

Lesson Objectives

Solve whole-number subtraction equations

Additional Examples

Example 1

Solve each equation. Check your answers.

A. $y - 23 = 39$

$y - 23 = \quad 39$ 23 is subtracted from y.

$\underline{+ 23} \quad \underline{+ 23}$ ☐ 23 to both sides to undo the

☐.

$y \quad = \quad$ ▨

Check $y - 23 = 39$

$62 - 23 \stackrel{?}{=} 39$ Substitute ☐ for y in the equation.

$39 \stackrel{?}{=} 39$ ✓   ☐ is the solution.

B. $78 = s - 15$

$78 = s - 15$ 15 is subtracted from s.

$\underline{+ 15} \quad \underline{+ 15}$ ☐ 15 to both sides to undo the

☐.

▨ $= s$

Check $78 = s - 15$

$78 \stackrel{?}{=} 93 - 15$ Substitute ☐ for s in the equation.

$78 \stackrel{?}{=} 78$ ✓   ☐ is the solution.

Copyright © by Holt McDougal.
All rights reserved.

Holt McDougal Mathematics

Solve the equation. Check your answer.

C. $z - 3 = 12$

$z - 3 = 12$ 3 is subtracted from z.

$\underline{+\ 3 \quad +\ 3}$ [____] 3 to both sides to undo the

[_____].

$z \quad = $ [____]

Check $z - 3 = 12$

$15 - 3 \overset{?}{=} 12$ Substitute [____] for z in the equation.

$12 \overset{?}{=} 12$ ✓   [____] is the solution.

Check It Out!

1. Solve the equation. Check your answer.

$57 = c - 13$

2. Solve the equation. Check your answer.

$g - 62 = 14$

Copyright © by Holt McDougal.
All rights reserved.

Holt McDougal Mathematics

Multiplication Equations

Lesson Objectives

Solve whole-number multiplication equations

Additional Examples

Example 1

Solve each equation. Check your answers.

A. $5p = 75$

$5p = 75$ p is multiplied by 5.

$\dfrac{5p}{5} = \dfrac{75}{5}$ [   ] both sides by 5 to undo the

[   ].

$p = $ [   ]

Check $5p = 75$

$5(15) \overset{?}{=} 75$ Substitute [   ] for p in the equation.

$75 \overset{?}{=} 75$ ✓   [   ] is the solution.

B. $16 = 8r$

$16 = 8r$ r is multiplied by 8.

$\dfrac{16}{8} = \dfrac{8r}{8}$ [   ] both sides by 8 to undo the

[   ].

 $= r$

Check $16 = 8r$

$16 \overset{?}{=} 8(2)$ Substitute [   ] for r in the equation.

$16 \overset{?}{=} 16$ ✓   [   ] is the solution.

Copyright © by Holt McDougal.
All rights reserved.

Holt McDougal Mathematics

Example 2 PROBLEM SOLVING APPLICATION

The area of a rectangle is 56 square inches. Its length is 8 inches. What is its width?

1. Understand the Problem

The answer will be the ☐ of the rectangle in inches.

List the important information:

- The area of the rectangle is ☐ square inches.

- The length of the rectangle is ☐ inches.

Draw a diagram to represent this information.

w

2. Make a Plan

You can write and solve an equation using the formula for area. To find the area of a rectangle, multiply its length by its width.

$A = lw$

$56 = 8w$

w

l

3. Solve

$56 = 8w$ w is multiplied by 8.

$\frac{56}{8} = \frac{8w}{8}$ ☐ both sides by 8 to undo the

☐

 $= w$

So the width of the rectangle is ☐ inches.

4. Look Back

Arrange 56 identical squares in a rectangle. The length is 8, so line up the squares in rows of 8. You can make 7 rows of 8, so the width is 7.

Copyright © by Holt McDougal.
All rights reserved.

Holt McDougal Mathematics

Check It Out!

1. Solve the equation. Check your answer.

$8a = 72$

2. Problem Solving Application

The area of a rectangle is 48 square inches. Its width is 6 inches. What is its length?

1. Understand the Problem

Draw a diagram to represent the important information.

2. Make a Plan

3. Solve

4. Look Back

Arrange 48 identical squares in a rectangle. The width is 6, so line up the squares in columns of 6. You can make ☐ columns of 6, so the length of the rectangle is ☐.

Copyright © by Holt McDougal.
All rights reserved.

Holt McDougal Mathematics

Division Equations

Lesson Objectives

Solve whole-number division equations

Additional Examples

Example 1

Solve each equation. Check your answers.

A. $\frac{x}{7} = 5$

$\frac{x}{7} = 5$ *x* is divided by 7.

$7 \cdot \frac{x}{7} = 7 \cdot 5$ ☐ both sides by 7 to undo the

☐ .

$x = $ ☐

Check $\frac{x}{7} = 5$

$\frac{35}{7} \overset{?}{=} 5$ Substitute ☐ for *x* in the equation.

$5 \overset{?}{=} 5 \checkmark$ ☐ is the solution.

B. $13 = \frac{p}{6}$

$13 = \frac{p}{6}$ *p* is divided by 6.

$6 \cdot 13 = 6 \cdot \frac{p}{6}$ ☐ both sides by 6 to undo the

☐ .

 $= p$

Check $13 = \frac{p}{6}$

$13 \overset{?}{=} \frac{78}{6}$ Substitute ☐ for *p* in the equation.

$13 \overset{?}{=} 13 \checkmark$ ☐ is the solution.

Copyright © by Holt McDougal.
All rights reserved.

Holt McDougal Mathematics

Example 2

At Elk Meadows Park an aspen tree is one-third the height of a pine tree.

$$\text{height of aspen} = \frac{\text{height of pine}}{3}$$

The aspen tree is 14 feet tall. How tall is the pine tree?

Let h represent the height of the pine tree.

$14 = \dfrac{h}{3}$ Substitute 14 for height of aspen. h is divided by 3.

$3 \cdot 14 = 3 \cdot \dfrac{h}{3}$ ⬚ both sides by 3 to undo the ⬚.

⬚ $= h$

The pine tree is ⬚ feet tall.

Check It Out!

1. Solve the equation. Check your answer.

$72 = \dfrac{p}{4}$

2. Jamie weighs one-half as much as her father.

$$\text{Jamie's weight} = \frac{\text{father's weight}}{2}$$

Jamie weighs 95 pounds. How many pounds does her father weigh?

Copyright © by Holt McDougal.
All rights reserved.

Holt McDougal Mathematics

Chapter Review

2-1 Variables and Expressions

Evaluate each expression to find the missing values in the tables.

1.

m	$32 + m$
18	50
28	?
38	?

2.

n	$4 \times n + 15$
4	31
5	?
6	?

3. Laura's journal can fit 60 words on a page. How many words does Laura have if she fills 3, 4, 5, or 6 pages?

2-2 Translating Between Words and Math

Write each phrase as a numerical or algebraic expression.

4. 218 less than 345

5. the product of 5 and k

6. the sum of b and 98

Write two phrases for each expression.

7. $563 + 72$

8. $y \div 13$

9. $18p$

10. Let z represent the number of hours for which Kendall must do homework every night he has school. Write an expression for the number of hours for which Kendall must do homework in a week in which he had school Monday through Friday.

11. Let m represent the number of miles Skyler jogs every week. Write an expression for the number of miles Skyler jogs per day.

Copyright © by Holt McDougal.
All rights reserved.

Holt McDougal Mathematics

2-3 Translating Between Tables and Expressions

Write an expression for the missing value in the table.

12.

Bicycles	1	2	3	n
Wheels	2	4	6	?

Write an expression for the sequence in the table.

13.

Position	1	2	3	4	5	n
Value of Term	14	15	16	17	18	?

2-4 Equations and Their Solutions

Determine whether the given value of each variable is a solution.

14. $46 + t = 63$
for $t = 27$

15. $7u = 42$
for $u = 6$

16. $d - 26 = 12$
for $d = 38$

17. Ty bought 7 pens and should get $2.25 back in change. The cashier gave him 10 quarters. Determine if Ty was given the correct amount of change. Explain.

2-5 Addition Equations

Solve each equation. Check your answers.

18. $h + 34 = 87$

19. $79 = 61 + v$

20. $46 = d + 12$

21. A high school library has fiction and non-fiction books. There are 2,730 fiction books. The library has 7,680 books altogether. Write and solve an equation to find the number of non-fiction books in the high school library.

22. The drama club sold 596 tickets to the play. There were 387 people at the play on Friday. How many people were at the play on Saturday? Write and solve an equation to find the number of people at the play on Saturday.

Copyright © by Holt McDougal.
All rights reserved.

Holt McDougal Mathematics

2-6 Subtraction Equations

Solve each equation. Check your answers.

23. $r - 17 = 7$

24. $180 = 220 - k$

25. $74 - l = 59$

26. A football field is 100 yards long. A football team is on their own 34-yard line. Write and solve an equation to find the number of yards the team must go to score a touchdown.

2-7 Multiplication Equations

Solve each equation. Check your answers.

27. $7j = 28$

28. $125 = 5f$

29. $77 = 7w$

30. Corban bought 4 CDs for $60. Each CD cost the same amount. Write and solve an equation to find the amount Corban spent per CD.

2-8 Division Equations

Solve each equation. Check your answers.

31. $10 = \dfrac{t}{6}$

32. $\dfrac{x}{5} = 8$

33. $6 = \dfrac{p}{8}$

34. Franz baked four dozen cookies for a bake sale. Each dozen cookies required three cups of chocolate chips. Write and solve an equation to find out how many cups of chocolate chips Franz bought.

Copyright © by Holt McDougal.
All rights reserved.

Holt McDougal Mathematics

Big Ideas

Answer these question to summarize the important concepts from Chapter 2 in your own words.

1. Explain what it means to evaluate an expression with values of a variable.

2. When translating from words to math, there are key words that represent each operation. List two key words that represent addition. List two keys words for subtraction. List two key words for multiplication. List two key words for division.

3. What does it mean to be a solution of an equation?

4. Explain how to solve a whole-number equation.

For more review of Chapter 2:

- Complete the Chapter 2 Study Guide and Review on pages 88–90 of your textbook.

- Complete the Ready to Go On quizzes on pages 64 and 84 of your textbook.

Copyright © by Holt McDougal.
All rights reserved.

Holt McDougal Mathematics

Representing, Comparing, and Ordering Decimals

Lesson Objectives

Write, compare, and order decimals using place value and number lines

Additional Examples

Example 1

Write each decimal in standard form, expanded form, and words.

A. 1.07

Expanded form: 1 + [ ]

Word form: one and seven [ ]

B. 0.03 + 0.006 + 0.0009

Standard form: [ ]

Word form: three hundred sixty-nine [ ]

Example 2

The star Wolf 359 has an apparent magnitude of 13.5. Suppose another star has an apparent magnitude of 13.05. Which star has the smaller magnitude?

1 3.5 0   Line up the decimal points.

1 3.0 5   Start from the [ ] and compare the digits.

Look for the [ ] place where the digits are different.

0 is less than 5.

[ ] < [ ]

The star that has an apparent magnitude of [ ] has the smaller magnitude.

Copyright © by Holt McDougal.
All rights reserved.

Holt McDougal Mathematics

Example 3

Order the decimals from least to greatest.
16.67, 16.6, 16.07

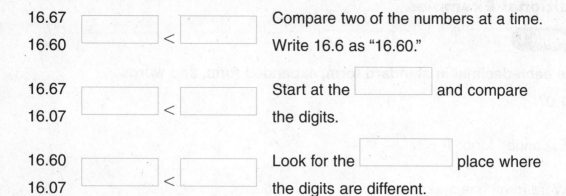

16.67
16.60
[ ] < [ ]
Compare two of the numbers at a time.
Write 16.6 as "16.60."

16.67
16.07
[ ] < [ ]
Start at the [ ] and compare the digits.

16.60
16.07
[ ] < [ ]
Look for the [ ] place where the digits are different.

Graph the numbers on a number line.

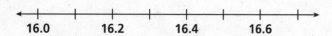

16.0   16.2   16.4   16.6

The numbers are ordered when you read the number line from left to right.

The numbers from least to greatest are [ ] , [ ] , and [ ] .

Check It Out!

1. Write the decimal in standard form and expanded form.

   eleven and two hundredths

   [ ]

2. Tina reported on a star for her science project that has a magnitude of 11.3. Maven reported on another star that has a magnitude of 11.03. Which star has the smaller magnitude?

   [ ]

3. Order the decimals from least to greatest.

   12.42, 12.4, 12.02

   [ ]

Copyright © by Holt McDougal.
All rights reserved.

Holt McDougal Mathematics

Estimating Decimals

Lesson Objectives

Estimate decimal sums, differences, products, and quotients

Vocabulary

clustering (p. 104) _____

_____

front-end estimation (p. 105) _____

_____

Additional Examples

Example 1

Nancy wants to cycle, ice skate, and water ski for 30 minutes each. About how many calories will she burn in all? (Cycling = 165.5 calories, ice skating = 177.5 calories, and water skiing = 171.5 calories.)

165.5 → 170   The addends [   ] around 170.

177.5 → 170   To estimate the total number of calories,

+ 171.5 → + 170   [   ] each addend to 170. Add.

[   ]

Nancy burns about [   ] calories.

Copyright © by Holt McDougal.
All rights reserved.

Holt McDougal Mathematics

Example 2

Estimate by rounding to the indicated place value.

A. 7.13 + 4.68; ones

7.13 + 4.68   Round to the nearest ☐ number.

☐ + ☐ = ☐   The sum is about ▢.

B. 9.705 − 0.2683; tenths

9.705   9.7   Round to the ☐.

− 0.2683   − 0.3   Align the ☐.

▢   Subtract.

Example 3

Estimate each product or quotient.

A. 33.83 × 1.98

35 × 2 = ▢   ☐ and ☐ are compatible.

So 33.83 × 1.98 is about ▢.

B. 72.77 ÷ 26.14

75 ÷ 25 = ▢   ☐ and ☐ are compatible.

So 72.77 ÷ 26.14 is about ▢.

Copyright © by Holt McDougal.
All rights reserved.

Holt McDougal Mathematics

Example 4

Estimate a range for the sum.

7.86 + 36.97 + 5.40

7.86 ➛ 7   Add the ☐ numbers only.

36.97 ➛ 36   The whole-number values of the decimals are

+ 5.40 ➛ + 5   ☐ than the actual numbers, so the answer

at least ☐   is an ☐ .

The exact answer of 7.86 + 36.97 + 5.40 is ☐ or greater.

You can estimate a range for the sum by adjusting the decimal part of the numbers. Round the decimals to 0, 0.5, or 1.

0.86 ➛ 1.00   Add the ☐ part of the

0.97 ➛ 1.00   numbers.

+ 0.40 ➛ + 0.50   Add the whole-number estimate and the

☐   ☐ estimate.

48.00 + 2.5 = ☐   The adjusted decimals are greater than the

actual decimal, so 50.50 is an

☐ .

The estimated range for the sum is from ☐ to ☐ .

Copyright © by Holt McDougal.
All rights reserved.

Holt McDougal Mathematics

Check It Out!

1. Abner wants to run, roller-skate, and snow ski for 60 minutes each. About how many calories will he burn in all? (Running = 185.5 calories, roller-skating = 189.5 calories, and snow skiing = 191.5 calories.)

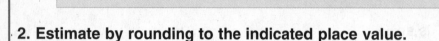

2. Estimate by rounding to the indicated place value.

   6.09 + 3.72; ones

3. Estimate the product or quotient.

   62.31 ÷ 18.52

4. Estimate a range for the sum.

   8.92 + 47.88 + 3.41

Copyright © by Holt McDougal.
All rights reserved.

Holt McDougal Mathematics

LESSON 3-3 — Adding and Subtracting Decimals

Lesson Objectives

Add and subtract decimals

Additional Examples

Example 1

Carly Patterson's Preliminary Scores	
Event	Points
Floor exercise	9.7
Balance beam	9.7
Vault	9.3
Uneven bars	9.45

A. What was Carly Patterson's total for the events other than the floor exercise?

Find the sum of 9.7, 9.3, and 9.45.

9.7 + 9.3 + 9.45   Estimate by rounding to the nearest whole number.

10 + 9 + 9 = ☐   The total is about ☐ points.

9.70   Align the ☐ points.
9.30
+ 9.45   Use ☐ as placeholders.

☐   Add. Then place the decimal point.

Since ☐ is close to the estimate of 28, the answer is

reasonable. Carly Patterson's total for the events other than the floor exercise

was ☐.

Copyright © by Holt McDougal. All rights reserved. Holt McDougal Mathematics

B. How many more points did Carly need on the vault to have a perfect score?

Find the difference between 10 and [   ].

10.0   Align the [   ] points.

− 9.3   Use [   ] as placeholders.

[   ]   Subtract. Then place the decimal point.

Carly needed another [   ] points to have a perfect score.

Example 2

Find each sum or difference.

A. 1.8 + 0.2

1.8 + 0.2 = [   ]   Think: 0.8 + 0.2 = [   ].

B. 4 − 0.7

4 − 0.7 = [   ]   Think: What number added to [   ] is 1?

0.7 + [   ] = 1

So 1 − 0.7 = [   ].

Example 3

Evaluate 6.73 − *x* for each value of *x*.

A. *x* = 3.8

6.73 − *x*

6.73 − [   ]   Substitute [   ] for *x*.

6.73   Align the decimal points.

− 3.80   Use a [   ] as a placeholder.

Subtract. Place the decimal point.

[   ]

Copyright © by Holt McDougal.
All rights reserved.

Holt McDougal Mathematics

B. $x = 2.9765$

$6.73 - x$

$6.73 -$ [   ]   Substitute [   ] for x.

   6.7300   Align the decimal points.

$-\ 2.9765$ Use [   ] as placeholders.

                    Subtract. Place the decimal point.

[   ]

Check It Out!

1. What was Carly Patterson's total for the events other than the vault exercise?

[   ]

2. Find the difference.

$6 - 0.3$

3. Evaluate $7.58 - x$ for the value of x.

$x = 3.8$

Copyright © by Holt McDougal.
All rights reserved.

Holt McDougal Mathematics

LESSON 3-4

Scientific Notation

Know it!
Note

Lesson Objectives

Write large numbers in scientific notation

Vocabulary

scientific notation (p. 124) _____

_____

Additional Examples

Example 1

Find each product.

A. 5,892 × 1,000 　　There are ☐ zeros in 1,000.

5,892,000 　　To multiply, move the decimal point ☐ places to

the ☐ .

= ▭ 　　Write ☐ placeholder zeros.

B. 47.75 × 10,000 　　There are ☐ zeros in 10,000.

47.7500 　　To multiply, move the decimal point ☐ places to

the ☐ .

= ▭ 　　Write ☐ placeholder zeros.

Example 2

Write 6,000,000 in scientific notation.

6,000,000 　　Move the decimal point ☐ places ▭ .

The power of 10 is ☐ .

6,000,000 = ▭

Copyright © by Holt McDougal.
All rights reserved.

Holt McDougal Mathematics

Example 3

Write 6.2174 × 10³ in standard form.

6.2174×10^3 The power of 10 is $\boxed{}$.

6.2174 Move the decimal point $\boxed{}$ places $\boxed{}$.

$6.2174 \times 10^3 = \boxed{}$

Example 4

Write the distance to the Sun, 93,000,000 miles, in scientific notation.

93,000,000   Move the decimal point $\boxed{}$ to form a number

greater than $\boxed{}$ and less than $\boxed{}$.

93,000,000   Multiply that number by a power of $\boxed{}$.

$\boxed{}$ The power of 10 is $\boxed{}$, because the decimal point is

moved $\boxed{}$ places left.

The distance to the sun is $\boxed{}$ miles.

Check It Out!

1. Find the product.

   $52.91 \times 10,000$

2. Write 8,000,000 in scientific notation.

3. Write 9.77 × 10⁵ in standard form.

Copyright © by Holt McDougal.
All rights reserved.

Holt McDougal Mathematics

Multiplying Decimals

Lesson Objectives

Multiply decimals by whole numbers and by decimals

Additional Examples

Example 1

Something that weighs 1 lb on Earth weighs 0.17 lb on the Moon. How much would a 4 lb dumbbell weigh on the Moon?

4×0.17

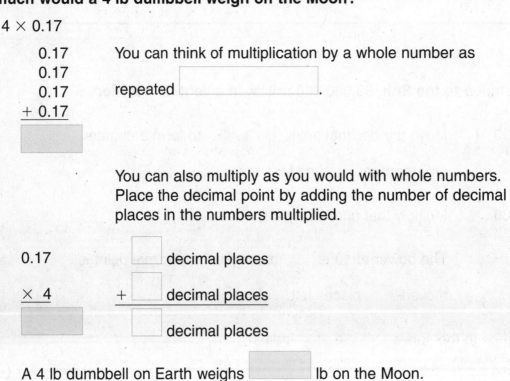

```
  0.17
  0.17       You can think of multiplication by a whole number as
  0.17
+ 0.17       repeated _____.
[        ]
```

You can also multiply as you would with whole numbers. Place the decimal point by adding the number of decimal places in the numbers multiplied.

```
  0.17        [  ]  decimal places
× 4        +  [  ]  decimal places
[      ]      [  ]  decimal places
```

A 4 lb dumbbell on Earth weighs [   ] lb on the Moon.

Copyright © by Holt McDougal.
All rights reserved.

Holt McDougal Mathematics

Example 2

Find each product.

A. 0.3×0.4

Multiply. Then place the decimal point.

0.3

$\times$ 0.4

[____]

[____] decimal place

$+$ [____] decimal place

[____] decimal places

Find each product.

B. 0.07×0.8

$0.07 \times 1 =$ [____]

Estimate the product. [____] is close to 1.

Multiply. Then place the decimal point.

0.07

$\times$ 0.8

[____]

[____] decimal places

$+$ [____] decimal place

[____] decimal places; use a placeholder zero

[____] is close to the estimate of [____].

The answer is reasonable.

C. 1.34×2.5

$1 \times 3 = 3$

Estimate the product. Round each factor to the nearest [____] number.

Multiply. Then place the decimal point.

1.34

$\times$ 2.5

670

2680

[____]

[____] decimal places

$+$ [____] decimal place

[____] decimal places

[____] is close to the estimate of [____].

The answer is reasonable.

Copyright © by Holt McDougal.
All rights reserved.

Holt McDougal Mathematics

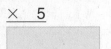

Example 3

Evaluate 5x for each value of x.

A. x = 3.062

5x = 5([_____])   Substitute [_____] for x.

$$
\begin{array}{r}
3.062 \\
\times \quad 5 \\
\hline
\end{array}
$$

[__] decimal places

+ [__] decimal places

[__] decimal places

B. x = 4.79

5x = 5([_____])   Substitute [_____] for x.

$$
\begin{array}{r}
4.79 \\
\times \quad 5 \\
\hline
\end{array}
$$

[__] decimal places

+ [__] decimal places

[__] decimal places

Check It Out!

1. Something that weighs 1 lb on Earth weighs 0.17 lb on the Moon. How much would a 7 lb dumbbell weigh on the Moon?

2. Find the product.

3.80 × 3.3

3. Evaluate 5x for the value of x.

x = 6.22

Copyright © by Holt McDougal.
All rights reserved.

Holt McDougal Mathematics

Dividing Decimals by Whole Numbers

Lesson Objectives

Divide decimals by whole numbers

Additional Examples

Example 1

Find each quotient.

A. 0.84 ÷ 3

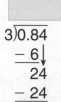

```
    ____
3)0.84
  − 6↓
   ─────
    24
  − 24
   ─────
     0
```

Place a decimal point in the ⬚ directly

above the decimal point in the ⬚. Divide as

you would with ⬚ numbers.

B. 3.56 ÷ 4

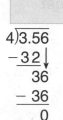

```
    ____
4)3.56
  −32↓
   ─────
    36
  − 36
   ─────
     0
```

Place a decimal point in the ⬚ directly

above the decimal point in the ⬚. Divide as

you would with ⬚.

Example 2

Evaluate 0.936 ÷ x for each given value of x.

A. x = 9

0.936 ÷ x

0.936 ÷ ⬚   Substitute ⬚ for x.

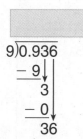

```
     _____
9)0.936
  − 9↓↓
   ──────
     3
   − 0↓
   ──────
    36
  − 36
   ──────
     0
```

Sometimes you need to use a ⬚ as a

placeholder.

9 > 3, so place a zero in the quotient and divide 9 into 36.

Copyright © by Holt McDougal.
All rights reserved.
Holt McDougal Mathematics

Evaluate 0.936 ÷ x for each given value of x.

B. $x = 18$

0.936 ÷ x

0.936 ÷ ☐   Substitute ☐ for x.

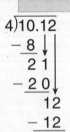

18)0.936
  − 0↓|
     93|
  − 90↓
     36
  − 36
      0

Sometimes you need to use a ☐ as a

placeholder.

$18 > 9$, so place a zero in the quotient and divide 18 into 93.

Example 3

Jodi and three of her friends are making a tile design. The materials cost $10.12. If they share the cost equally, how much should each person pay?

$10.12 should be divided into four equal groups.

Divide $10.12 by ☐ .

4)10.12
  − 8 ↓
    2 1
  − 2 0↓
      12
  − 12
      0

Place a ☐ in the quotient directly above the decimal point in the dividend.

Divide as you would with whole numbers.

Each person should pay ☐ .

Check It Out!

1. Find the quotient.

2.96 ÷ 4

Copyright © by Holt McDougal.
All rights reserved.

Holt McDougal Mathematics

Dividing by Decimals

Lesson Objectives

Divide whole numbers and decimals by decimals

Additional Examples

Example 1

Find each quotient.

A. $5.2 \div 1.3$

$1.3 \overline{)5.2}$ Multiply the divisor and dividend by the same power of ten.

There is [   ] decimal place in the divisor.

$13 \overline{)52}$
$\underline{-52}$
0

Multiply by 10^1, or [   ].

Think: $1.3 \times 10 =$ [   ] $5.2 \times 10 =$ [   ]

Divide.

B. $61.3 \div 0.36$

$0.36 \overline{)61.30}$ Make the divisor a [   ] by multiplying

the divisor and dividend by [   ], or [   ].

$36 \overline{)6130.00}$
$\underline{-36}$
253
$\underline{-252}$
100
$\underline{-72}$
280
$\underline{-252}$
28

Place the [   ] in the quotient.

Divide.

When there is a remainder, place a [   ] after the decimal point in the dividend and continue to divide.

$61.3 \div 0.36 =$ [   ]

Copyright © by Holt McDougal.
All rights reserved.

Holt McDougal Mathematics

Example 2 PROBLEM SOLVING APPLICATION

After driving 216.3 miles, the Yorks filled up with 10.5 gal of gas. On average, how many miles did they drive per gallon of gas?

1. Understand the Problem

The answer will be the average number of miles per gallon.
List the important information:

They drove [　　　] miles. They used [　　　] gallons of gas.

2. Make a Plan

Solve a simpler problem by replacing the decimals in the problem with whole numbers.

If they drove 10 miles using 2 gallons of gas, they averaged 5 miles per gallon. You need to divide [　　　] by [　　　] to solve the problem.

3. Solve

10.5)216.3   Multiply the divisor and dividend by 10.

105)2,163.0   Think: 10.5 × 10 = [　　　]   216.3 × 10 = [　　　]
− 210↓
    63   Place the decimal point in the quotient. Divide.
  − 0↓
   630
 − 630
    0

The York family averaged [　　　] miles per gallon.

4. Look Back

Use compatible numbers to estimate the quotient.

216.3 ÷ 10.5 ⟶ 220 ÷ 11 = 20

The answer is reasonable since 20.6 is close to the estimate of 20.

Copyright © by Holt McDougal.
All rights reserved.

Holt McDougal Mathematics

Check It Out!

1. Find the quotient.

    $51.2 \div 0.24$

2. Problem Solving Application
After driving 191.1 miles, the Changs used 10.5 gallons of gas. On average, how many miles did they drive per gallon of gas?

  1. Understand the Problem
    The answer will be the average number of miles per gallon.

    List the important information:

    They drove [＿＿＿] miles. They used [＿＿＿] gallons of gas.

  2. Make a Plan
    Solve a simpler problem by replacing the decimals in the problem with whole numbers.

    If they drove 10 miles using 2 gallons of gas, they averaged 5 miles per gallon. You need to divide [＿＿＿] by [＿＿＿] to solve the problem.

  3. Solve

  4. Look Back
    Use compatible numbers to estimate the quotient.

    $191.1 \div 10.5 \longrightarrow 190 \div 10 = 19$

    The answer is reasonable since 18.2 is close to the estimate of 19.

Copyright © by Holt McDougal.
All rights reserved.

Holt McDougal Mathematics

Interpreting the Quotient

Lesson Objectives

Solve problems by interpreting the quotient

Additional Examples

Example 1

Suppose Mark wants to make bags of slime. If each bag of slime requires 0.15 kg of corn starch and he has 1.23 kg, how many bags of slime can he make?

The question asks how many whole bags of slime can be made when the corn starch is divided into groups of 0.15 kg.

$1.23 \div 0.15 =$ ☐

Think: The quotient shows that there is not enough to make ☐ bags of slime that are 0.15 kg each. There is only enough for ☐ bags. The decimal part of the quotient will not be used in the answer.

Mark can make ☐ bags of slime.

Example 2

There are 237 students in the seventh grade. If Mr. Jones buys rolls of film with 36 exposures each, how many rolls will he need to take every student's picture?

The question asks how many rolls are needed to take a picture of every one of the students.

$237 \div 36 =$ ☐

Think: ☐ rolls of film will not be enough to take every student's picture.

Mr. Jones will need to buy another roll of film. The quotient must be rounded up to the next highest ☐ number.

Mr. Jones will need ☐ rolls of film.

Copyright © by Holt McDougal.
All rights reserved.

Holt McDougal Mathematics

Example 3

Gary has 42.25 meters of rope. If he cuts it into 13 equal pieces, how long is each piece?

The question asks exactly how long each section will be when the rope is cut into 13 equal pieces.

$42.25 \div 13 = \boxed{}$

Think: The question asks for an exact answer; so do not estimate. Use the entire quotient.

Each piece will be $\boxed{}$ meters long.

Check It Out!

1. **Suppose Antonio wants to make bags of slime. If each bag of slime requires 0.15 kg of corn starch and he has 1.44 kg, how many bags of slime can he make?**

2. **There are 342 students in the seventh grade. If Ms. Tia buys rolls of film with 24 exposures each, how many rolls will she need to take every student's picture?**

3. **Ethan has 64.20 meters of rope. If he cuts it into 15 equal pieces, how long is each piece?**

Copyright © by Holt McDougal.
All rights reserved.

Holt McDougal Mathematics

Solving Decimal Equations

Lesson Objectives

Solve equations involving decimals

Additional Examples

Example 1

Solve each equation. Check your answer.

A. $k - 6.2 = 9.5$

$k - 6.2 = 9.5$ 6.2 is subtracted from k.

$\underline{+ 6.2 \quad + 6.2}$ Add ☐ to both sides to undo the ☐.

$k = $ ☐

Check $k - 6.2 = 9.5$

$15.7 - 6.2 \overset{?}{=} 9.5$ Substitute ☐ for k in the equation.

$9.5 \overset{?}{=} 9.5$ ✓   ☐ is the solution.

B. $6k = 7.2$

$6k = 7.2$ k is multiplied by 6.

$\dfrac{6k}{6} = \dfrac{7.2}{6}$ Divide both sides by ☐ to undo the ☐.

$k = $ ☐

Check $6k = 7.2$

$6(1.2) \overset{?}{=} 7.2$ Substitute ☐ for k in the equation.

$7.2 \overset{?}{=} 7.2$ ✓   ☐ is the solution.

Copyright © by Holt McDougal.
All rights reserved.

Holt McDougal Mathematics

Solve the equation. Check your answer.

C. $\frac{m}{7} = 0.6$

$\frac{m}{7} = 0.6$ m is divided by 7.

$\frac{m}{7} \cdot 7 = 0.6 \cdot 7$ Multiply both sides by ⬚ to undo the ⬚.

$m = $ ▨

Check $\frac{m}{7} = 0.6$

$\frac{4.2}{7} \overset{?}{=} 0.6$ Substitute ⬚ for m in the equation.

$0.6 \overset{?}{=} 0.6$ ✓   ⬚ is the solution.

Example 2

A. The area of Emily's floor is 33.75 m². If its length is 4.5 meters, what is its width?

area = length · width

⬚ = ⬚ · w Write the equation for the problem.

$33.75 = 4.5w$ Let w be the ⬚ of the room.

$\frac{33.75}{4.5} = \frac{4.5w}{4.5}$ w is multiplied by ⬚.

▨ = w Divide both sides by ⬚ to undo the multiplication.

The width of the floor is ▨ meters.

Copyright © by Holt McDougal.
All rights reserved.

Holt McDougal Mathematics

B. If carpet costs \$23 per m², what is the total cost to carpet the floor?

total cost = area · cost of carpet per square meter

$C = \boxed{} \cdot 23$ Let $\boxed{}$ be the $\boxed{}$.
Write the equation for the problem.

$C = \boxed{}$ Multiply.

The total cost of carpeting the floor is $\boxed{}$.

Check It Out!

1. Solve the equation. Check your answer.

$$\frac{w}{9} = 0.3$$

2. The area of Yvonne's bedroom is 181.25 ft². If its length is 12.5 feet, what is its width?

Copyright © by Holt McDougal.
All rights reserved.

Holt McDougal Mathematics

CHAPTER 3

Chapter Review

3-1 Representing, Comparing, and Ordering Decimals

Write each number in words.

1. 7.09

2. 125.856

Order the numbers from greatest to least.

3. 24.428, 24.4285, 23.4389

4. 2.04, 2.004, 2.404, 2.4

3-2 Estimating Decimals

Estimate each by rounding to the indicated place value.

5. 8.497 − 1.346; tenths

6. 14.8557 + 11.7391; hundredths

Estimate each product or quotient.

7. 7.83 × 2.692

8. 18.237 ÷ 5.914

9. 28.652 ÷ 4.836

10. Ruthie bought 3 packages of ground beef, weighing 1.8 pounds, 2.2 pounds and 3.6 pounds. The beef costs $3.59 per pound. Estimate the total cost.

3-3 Adding and Subtracting Decimals

11. Kristy bought a birthday card for $2.95, a book for $12.29, and wrapping paper for $1.15. She paid with a $20 bill. How much change should she get back?

Add or subtract.

12. 3.73 + 7.29

13. 12.628 − 7.563

14. 32.876 + 14.69

Copyright © by Holt McDougal.
All rights reserved.

63

Holt McDougal Mathematics

3-4 Scientific Notation

Write each number in standard form.

15. 4.592×10^5 **16.** 2.47×10^3 **17.** 9.40×10^2

18. Mumbai, India is the most populated city in the world with a population of 11,914,398. Round the population to the nearest hundred thousand. Then write that number in scientific notation.

3-5 Multiplying Decimals

Find each product.

19.   0.07   **20.**   0.42   **21.** 0.007×0.06 **22.** 3.0×0.0009
       $\times\ 0.8$ $\times\ 0.09$

Evaluate.

23. $5t - 12 + t$ for $t = 4.6$ **24** $6^3 + 8p + p$ for $p = 0.39$

25. A piece of ribbon 3.2 inches in length is needed to make a small bow. How much ribbon is needed to make three small bows?

3-6 Dividing Decimals by Whole Numbers

Evaluate $x \div 6$ for each given value of x.

26. $x = 35.19$ **27.** $x = 6.312$ **28.** $x = 0.354$ **29.** $x = 0.846$

Find the value of each expression.

30. $(0.035 + 0.27) \div 5$ **31.** $(8.5 - 4.175) \div 5$ **32.** $(15.78 - 9.3) \div 8$

33. Four friends went to dinner. The bill was $63.60. They split the bill evenly. How much did each friend pay?

Copyright © by Holt McDougal.
All rights reserved.

Holt McDougal Mathematics

3-7 Dividing by Decimals

Divide.

34. $14.4 \div 0.6$

35. $45.612 \div 1.4$

36. $0.9132 \div 0.06$

Evaluate.

37. $0.66 \div c$ for $c = 0.04$

38. $y \div 3.28$ for $y = 22.468$

39. Ryan and his family drove 447.3 miles using 14.2 gallons of gasoline. On average, how many miles did they drive per gallon of gas?

3-8 Interpreting the Quotient

40. Marisa needs 105 thank-you cards for her graduation party guests. The cards come in packages of 12. How many packages will she need to buy?

41. There are 907 g in a box of pancake mix. Each serving size is 60 g. How many servings are in one box?

42. Cady's dog, Blitz, eats 2.75 cups of dog food each day. There are 88 cups of dog food in a bag. How many days will the bag of dog food last?

3-9 Solving Decimal Equations

Solve each equation. Check your answer.

43. $3.2 = \dfrac{m}{7}$

44. $7.4f = 44.4$

45. $z - 53.56 = 11.093$

46. Jeremy read his book at a rate of 13.4 pages per hour. At this rate, how many pages will he read in 8 hours?

Copyright © by Holt McDougal.
All rights reserved.

Holt McDougal Mathematics

Answer these questions to summarize the important concepts from Chapter 3 in your own words.

1. Explain how to compare two decimals.

2. List methods used to estimate the answer to decimal computation problems.

3. List the steps when adding or subtracting decimals.

4. What determines the power of 10, when a number is written in scientific notation?

5. List the steps when dividing by decimals.

For more review of Chapter 3:

- Complete the Chapter 3 Study Guide and Review on pages 144–146.

- Complete the Ready to Go On quizzes on pages 114 and 140.

Copyright © by Holt McDougal.
All rights reserved.

Holt McDougal Mathematics

Divisibility

Lesson Objectives

Use divisibility rules

Vocabulary

divisible (p. 156) _____

_____

composite number (p. 157) _____

_____

prime number (p. 157) _____

Additional Examples

Example 1

A. Tell whether 462 is divisible by 2, 3, 4, and 5.

2	The last digit, 2, is [ ].	Divisible
3	The sum of the digits is 4 + 6 + 2 = 12. 12 is divisible by [ ].	Divisible
4	The last two digits form the number 62. 62 is not divisible by [ ].	Not divisible
5	The last digit is 2.	Not divisible

So 462 is divisible by [   ] and [   ].

Copyright © by Holt McDougal.
All rights reserved.

Holt McDougal Mathematics

B. Tell whether 540 is divisible by 6, 9, and 10.

6	The number is divisible by both ☐ and ☐.	Divisible
9	The sum of the digits is 5 + 4 + 0 = 9. 9 is divisible by ☐.	Divisible
10	The last digit is ☐.	Divisible

So 540 is divisible by ☐, ☐, and ☐.

Example 2

Tell whether each number is prime or composite.

A. 23 divisible by ☐ ☐

B. 48 divisible by ☐ ☐

C. 31 divisible by ☐ ☐

D. 18 divisible by ☐ ☐

Check It Out!

1. Tell whether 114 is divisible by 2, 3, 4, and 5.

2. Tell whether the number is prime or composite.

27

Copyright © by Holt McDougal.
All rights reserved.

Holt McDougal Mathematics

Factors and Prime Factorization

Lesson Objectives

Write prime factorizations of composite numbers

Vocabulary

factor (p. 161) _____

_____

prime factorization (p. 161) _____

_____

Additional Examples

Example 1

List all of the factors of the number.

A. 16

Begin listing factors in pairs.

$16 = 1 \cdot 16$	1 is a factor.
$16 = 2 \cdot 8$	2 is a factor.
	3 is not a factor.
$16 = 4 \cdot 4$	4 is a factor.
	5 is not a factor.
	6 is not a factor.
	7 is not a factor.
$16 = 8 \cdot 2$	8 and 2 have already been listed, so stop here.

The factors of 16 are ⬚⬚⬚⬚⬚.

B. 19

$19 = \boxed{} \cdot \boxed{}$ Begin listing factors in pairs.
19 is not divisible by any other whole numbers.

The factors of 19 are ⬚⬚⬚⬚⬚.

Copyright © by Holt McDougal.
All rights reserved.

Holt McDougal Mathematics

Example 2

Write the prime factorization of each number.

A. 24

Method 1: Use a factor tree.

Choose any two factors of 24 to begin. Keep finding factors until each branch ends at a prime factor.

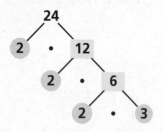   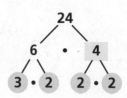

24 = [   ]   24 = [   ]

The prime factorization of 24 is [   ], or [   ].

B. 45

Method 2: Use a ladder diagram.

Choose a prime factor of 45 to begin. Keep dividing by prime factors until the quotient is 1.

3|45   3|45
3|15   3|15
5|5   5|5
1   1

45 = [   ]   45 = [   ]

The prime factorization of 45 is [   ] or [   ].

Check It Out!

1. List all factors of the number.

12

[   ]

Copyright © by Holt McDougal.
All rights reserved.

Holt McDougal Mathematics

Greatest Common Factor

Lesson Objectives

Find the greatest common factor (GCF) of a set of numbers

Vocabulary

greatest common factor (GCF) (p. 165) _____

_____

Additional Examples

Example 1

Find the GCF of each set of numbers.

A. 28 and 42

Method 1: List the factors.

factors of 28: 1, 2, 4, 7, 14, 28   List all the factors.

factors of 42: 1, 2, 3, 6, 7, 14, 21, 42   Circle the [   ].

The GCF of 28 and 42 is [   ].

B. 18, 30, and 24

Method 2: Use the prime factorization.

$18 = 2 \cdot 3 \cdot 3$ Write the [   ]

                    of each number.

$30 = 2 \cdot 3 \cdot 5$

$24 = 2 \cdot 3 \cdot 2 \cdot 2$ Find the common [   ] factors.

$2 \cdot 3 = 6$ Find the [   ] of the common prime

                    factors.

The GCF of 18, 30, and 24 is [   ].

Example 2 **PROBLEM SOLVING APPLICATION**

Jenna has 16 red flowers and 24 yellow flowers. She wants to make bouquets with the same number of each color flower in each bouquet. What is the greatest number of bouquets she can make?

1. Understand the Problem

The answer will be the greatest number of bouquets 16 red flowers and 24 yellow flowers can form so that each bouquet has the same number of red flowers, and each bouquet has the same number of yellow flowers.

2. Make a Plan

You can make an organized list of the possible bouquets.

3. Solve

Red	Yellow	Bouquets
2	3	(RR YYY) (RR YYY) (RR YYY) (RR YYY) (RR YYY) (RR YYY) (RR YYY) (RR YYY) 16 red, 24 yellow: Every flower is in a bouquet ✓

The greatest number of bouquets Jenna can make is ▢.

4. Look Back

To form the largest number of bouquets, find the GCF of 16 and 24.

factors of 16: 1, 2, 4, 8, 16

factors of 24: 1, 2, 3, 4, 6, 8, 12, 24

The GCF of 16 and 24 is ▢.

Copyright © by Holt McDougal.
All rights reserved.

Holt McDougal Mathematics

Check It Out!

1. Find the GCF of the set of numbers.

40, 16, and 24

2. Problem Solving Application

Peter has 18 oranges and 27 pears. He wants to make fruit baskets with the same number of each fruit in each basket. What is the greatest number of fruit baskets he can make?

1. Understand the Problem

The answer will be the greatest number of fruit baskets 18 oranges and 27 pears can form so that each basket has the same number of oranges, and each basket has the same number of pears.

2. Make a Plan

You can make an organized list of the possible fruit baskets.

3. Solve

4. Look Back

To form the largest number of baskets, find the _____ of 18 and 27.

factors of 18: _____

factors of 27: _____

The GCF of 18 and 27 is _____ .

Copyright © by Holt McDougal.
All rights reserved.

Holt McDougal Mathematics

Decimals and Fractions

Lesson Objectives

Convert between decimals and fractions

Vocabulary

mixed number (p. 175) _____

_____

terminating decimal (p. 176) _____

_____

repeating decimal (p. 176) _____

_____

Additional Examples

Example 1

Write each decimal as a fraction or mixed number.

A. 0.67

    0.67   Identify the place value of the digit farthest to the ⬚.

    ▭   The 7 is in the ⬚ place, so use

                ⬚ as the denominator.

B. 5.9

    5.9   Identify the place value of the digit farthest to the ⬚.

    ▭   Write the whole number, ⬚.

                The 9 is in the ⬚ place, so use ⬚ as the

                denominator.

Copyright © by Holt McDougal.
All rights reserved.
Holt McDougal Mathematics

Example 2

Write each fraction or mixed number as a decimal.

A. $\frac{3}{20}$

$$20)\overline{3.00}$$
$$\underline{-20}$$
$$100$$
$$\underline{-100}$$
$$0$$

Divide ☐ by ☐.

Add zeros after the decimal point.

The remainder is 0.

$$\frac{3}{20} = \boxed{}$$

B. $6\frac{1}{3}$

$$\begin{array}{r} 0.333 \\ 3)\overline{1.000} \\ \underline{-9} \\ 10 \\ \underline{-9} \\ 10 \\ \underline{-9} \\ 1 \end{array}$$

Divide ☐ by ☐.

Add zeros after the decimal point.

The ☐ repeats in the quotient.

$$6\frac{1}{3} = \boxed{} = \boxed{}$$

Copyright © by Holt McDougal.
All rights reserved.

Holt McDougal Mathematics

Example 3

Order the fractions and decimal from least to greatest.

$\frac{3}{4}$, 0.8, $\frac{7}{10}$

First, rewrite the fractions as [   ].

$\frac{3}{4}$ = [   ] $\frac{7}{10}$ = [   ]

Order the three decimals.

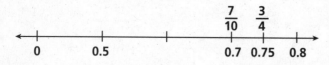

The numbers in order from least to greatest are [   ].

Check It Out!

1. Write the decimal as a mixed number.

4.8

2. Write the fraction as a decimal.

$\frac{5}{20}$

3. Order the fractions and decimal from least to greatest.

$\frac{1}{2}$, 0.35, $\frac{1}{4}$

Copyright © by Holt McDougal.
All rights reserved.

Holt McDougal Mathematics

Equivalent Fractions

Lesson Objectives

Write equivalent fractions

Vocabulary

equivalent fractions (p. 180) _____

_____

simplest form (p. 181) _____

_____

Additional Examples

Example 1

Find two equivalent fractions for $\frac{10}{12}$.

$$\frac{10}{12} \qquad = \qquad \boxed{} \qquad = \qquad \boxed{}$$

So $\frac{10}{12}$, ⬜ ,and ⬜ are all equivalent fractions.

Example 2

Find the missing number that makes the fractions equivalent.

A. $\frac{3}{5} = \frac{\blacksquare}{20}$

In the denominator, ⬜ is multiplied by ⬜ to get 20.

$\frac{3 \cdot 4}{5 \cdot 4} = \boxed{}$

Multiply the numerator, ⬜ , by the same number, ⬜ .

So $\frac{3}{5}$ is equivalent to ⬜ .

Copyright © by Holt McDougal.
All rights reserved.

Holt McDougal Mathematics

Find the missing number that makes the fractions equivalent.

B. $\frac{4}{5} = \frac{80}{\blacksquare}$

In the numerator, $\boxed{}$ is multiplied by $\boxed{}$ to get 80.

$\frac{4 \cdot 20}{5 \cdot 20} = \boxed{}$

Multiply the denominator, $\boxed{}$, by the same number, $\boxed{}$.

So $\frac{4}{5}$ is equivalent to $\boxed{}$.

Example 3

Write each fraction in simplest form.

A. $\frac{20}{48}$

The GCF of 20 and 48 is $\boxed{}$, so $\frac{20}{48}$ is not in simplest form.

Method 1: Use the GCF.

$\frac{20 \div 4}{48 \div 4} = \boxed{}$ Divide $\boxed{}$ and $\boxed{}$ by their GCF, $\boxed{}$.

B. $\frac{7}{10}$

The GCF of 7 and 10 is $\boxed{}$, so $\frac{7}{10}$ is already in simplest form.

Check It Out!

1. Find two equivalent fractions for $\frac{4}{6}$.

2. Find the missing number that makes the fractions equivalent.

$\frac{3}{9} = \frac{\blacksquare}{27}$

Mixed Numbers and Improper Fractions

Lesson Objectives

Convert between mixed numbers and improper fractions

Vocabulary

improper fraction (p. 186) _____

_____

proper fraction (p. 186) _____

_____

Additional Examples

Example 1

Ella hiked for $\frac{9}{4}$ hours yesterday. Write $\frac{9}{4}$ as a mixed number.

Method 1: Use a model.

Draw squares divided into fourth sections. Shade ☐ of the sections.

$\frac{1}{4}$	$\frac{1}{4}$
$\frac{1}{4}$	$\frac{1}{4}$

$\frac{1}{4}$	$\frac{1}{4}$
$\frac{1}{4}$	$\frac{1}{4}$

$\frac{1}{4}$	$\frac{1}{4}$
$\frac{1}{4}$	$\frac{1}{4}$

$\qquad$ 1 $\qquad$ 2 $\qquad$ $\frac{1}{4}$

There are ☐ whole squares and ☐ fourth square, or ☐ squares, shaded.

Method 2: Use division.

$$4\overline{)9}$$
$$\underline{-8}$$
$$1$$

Divide the numerator by the denominator.

To form the fraction part of the quotient, use the remainder

as the _____ and the divisor as the

_____.

Copyright © by Holt McDougal.
All rights reserved.

Holt McDougal Mathematics

Example 2

Write $3\frac{2}{3}$ as an improper fraction.

Method 1: Use a model.

You can draw a diagram to illustrate the whole and fractional parts.

There are ☐ thirds or ▯. Count the thirds in the diagram.

Method 2: Use multiplication and addition.

When you are changing a mixed number to an improper fraction, spiral clockwise as shown in the picture. The order of operations will help you remember to multiply before you add.

$$3\frac{2}{3} = \frac{(3 \cdot 3) + 2}{3}$$

$$= \frac{9 + 2}{3}$$

Multiply the ☐ number

by the ☐ and

add the ☐.

Keep the same ☐.

$$= ▯$$

Then add.

Multiply.

Check It Out!

1. Arnold biked for $\frac{7}{4}$ hours yesterday. Write $\frac{7}{4}$ as a mixed number.

2. Write $4\frac{1}{3}$ as an improper fraction.

Copyright © by Holt McDougal.
All rights reserved.

Holt McDougal Mathematics

Comparing and Ordering Fractions

Lesson Objectives

Use pictures and number lines to compare and order fractions

Vocabulary

like fractions (p. 192) _____

_____

unlike fractions (p. 192) _____

_____

common denominator (p. 192) _____

Additional Examples

Example 1

Compare. Write <, >, or =.

A. $\frac{6}{7}$ ◻ $\frac{4}{7}$

$$\frac{6}{7} \quad \square \quad \frac{4}{7}$$

From the model, $\frac{6}{7}$ 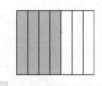 $\frac{4}{7}$.

B. $\frac{1}{9}$ ◻ $\frac{5}{9}$

$$\frac{1}{9} \quad \square \quad \frac{5}{9}$$

From the model, $\frac{1}{9}$ $\frac{5}{9}$.

Copyright © by Holt McDougal.
All rights reserved.

Holt McDougal Mathematics

Example 2

Ray has $\frac{2}{3}$ cup of nuts. He needs $\frac{3}{4}$ cup to make cookies. Does he have enough nuts for the recipe?

Compare $\frac{2}{3}$ and $\frac{3}{4}$.

Find a common denominator by ⬚ the denominators. $3 \times 4 =$ ⬚

Find equivalent fractions with ⬚ as the denominator.

$\frac{2}{3} = \frac{\blacksquare}{12}$ $\frac{3}{4} = \frac{\blacksquare}{12}$

$\frac{2 \cdot 4}{3 \cdot 4} = \frac{\square}{12}$ $\frac{3 \cdot 3}{4 \cdot 3} = \frac{\square}{12}$

$\frac{2}{3} = \frac{\square}{12}$ $\frac{3}{4} = \frac{\square}{12}$

Compare the like fractions. $\frac{8}{12}$ ⬚ $\frac{9}{12}$, so $\frac{2}{3}$ ⬚ $\frac{3}{4}$.

Since $\frac{2}{3}$ cup is ⬚ $\frac{3}{4}$ cup, he ▨ have enough.

Example 3

Order the fractions from least to greatest: $\frac{4}{5}$, $\frac{2}{3}$, and $\frac{1}{3}$

$\frac{4 \cdot 3}{5 \cdot 3} = $ ⬚ $\frac{2 \cdot 5}{3 \cdot 5} = $ ⬚ $\frac{1 \cdot 5}{3 \cdot 5} = $ ⬚   Rename with like denominators.

⬚   ⬚ ⬚

```
<---+--+--+--+--+--●--+--+--+--+--●--+--●--+--+--+--->
    0              1              2     4          1
                   ─              ─     ─
                   3              3     5
```

The fractions in order from least to greatest are ▨ , ▨ , ▨ .

Copyright © by Holt McDougal.
All rights reserved.

Holt McDougal Mathematics

Check It Out!

1. Compare. Write <, >, or =.

$$\frac{4}{6} \ \blacksquare \ \frac{5}{6}$$

2. Trevor has $\frac{1}{3}$ cup of soil. He needs $\frac{1}{4}$ cup to fill a small planter. Does he have enough soil to fill the planter?

3. Order the fractions from least to greatest: $\frac{4}{7}$, $\frac{3}{4}$, and $\frac{1}{4}$

Copyright © by Holt McDougal.
All rights reserved.

Holt McDougal Mathematics

Adding and Subtracting with Like Denominators

Lesson Objectives

Add and subtract fractions with like denominators

Additional Examples

Example 1

Snow was falling at a rate of $\frac{1}{4}$ inch per hour. How much snow fell after two hours? Write your answer in simplest form.

$\frac{1}{4} + \frac{1}{4}$

$\frac{1}{4} + \frac{1}{4} = \boxed{}$ Add the [   ]. Keep the same

[   ].

$= \boxed{}$ Write your answer in simplest form.

After 2 hours $\boxed{}$ inch of snow fell.

Example 2

Subtract. Write each answer in simplest form.

A. $1 - \frac{3}{5}$

To get a common denominator, rewrite 1 as a fraction

with a [   ] of [   ].

$\frac{5}{5} - \frac{3}{5} = \boxed{}$ Subtract the [   ]. Keep the same

[   ].

B. $5\frac{5}{12} - 2\frac{1}{12}$

$5\frac{5}{12} - 2\frac{1}{12}$ Subtract the [   ]. Then subtract the

[   ].

$\boxed{}$

$\boxed{}$ Write your answer in simplest form.

Copyright © by Holt McDougal.
All rights reserved.

Holt McDougal Mathematics

Example 3

Evaluate each expression for $x = \frac{2}{9}$. Write each answer in simplest form.

A. $\frac{5}{9} - x$

$\frac{5}{9} - x$ Write the expression.

$\frac{5}{9} - \frac{2}{9} = \boxed{}$ Substitute $\boxed{}$ for x and subtract the

$\boxed{}$.

Keep the same $\boxed{}$.

$= \boxed{}$ Write your answer in simplest form.

B. $x + 2\frac{4}{9}$

$x + 2\frac{4}{9}$ Write the expression.

$\frac{2}{9} + 2\frac{4}{9} = \boxed{}$ Substitute $\boxed{}$ for x and add the

$\boxed{}$.

Then add the $\boxed{}$ numbers.

$= \boxed{}$, or $\frac{8}{3}$ Write your answer in simplest form.

Check It Out!

1. Rain was falling at a rate of $\frac{1}{8}$ inch per hour. How much rain fell after two hours? Write your answer in simplest form.

2. Subtract. Write the answer in simplest form.

$1 - \frac{2}{6}$

Copyright © by Holt McDougal.
All rights reserved.

Holt McDougal Mathematics

Estimating Fraction Sums and Differences

Lesson Objectives

Estimate sums and differences of fractions and mixed numbers

Additional Examples

Example 1

Estimate each sum or difference by rounding to 0, $\frac{1}{2}$, or 1.

A. $\frac{6}{7} + \frac{3}{8}$

$\frac{6}{7} + \frac{3}{8}$

$\boxed{} + \boxed{} = \boxed{}$

Think: $\frac{6}{7}$ rounds to $\boxed{}$ and $\frac{3}{8}$ rounds to $\boxed{}$.

$\frac{6}{7} + \frac{3}{8}$ is about $\boxed{}$.

B. $\frac{9}{10} - \frac{7}{8}$

$\frac{9}{10} - \frac{7}{8}$

$\boxed{} - \boxed{} = 0$

Think: $\frac{9}{10}$ rounds to $\boxed{}$ and $\frac{7}{8}$ rounds to $\boxed{}$.

$\frac{9}{10} - \frac{7}{8}$ is about $\boxed{}$.

Example 2

The table shows the distances Tosha walked.

A. About how far did Tosha walk on Tuesday and Thursday?

$5\frac{1}{10} + 4\frac{7}{8}$

$\boxed{} + \boxed{} = \boxed{}$

She walked about $\boxed{}$ miles on Tuesday and Thursday.

Tosha's Walking Distances	
Day	**Distance (mi)**
Tuesday	$5\frac{1}{10}$
Thursday	$4\frac{7}{8}$
Saturday	$6\frac{3}{7}$
Sunday	$8\frac{9}{10}$

Copyright © by Holt McDougal.
All rights reserved.

Holt McDougal Mathematics

B. About how much farther did Tosha walk on Sunday than Thursday?

$$8\frac{9}{10} - 4\frac{7}{8}$$

$$\boxed{} - \boxed{} = \boxed{}$$

She walked about ▭ miles farther on Sunday than on Thursday.

C. Estimate the total distance Tosha walked on Thursday, Saturday, and Sunday.

$$4\frac{7}{8} + 6\frac{3}{7} + 8\frac{9}{10}$$

$$\boxed{} + \boxed{} + \boxed{} = \boxed{}$$

She walked about ▭ miles on Thursday, Saturday, and Sunday.

Check It Out!

1. Estimate each sum or difference by rounding to 0, $\frac{1}{2}$, or 1.

$$\frac{5}{6} + \frac{3}{7}$$

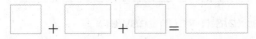

2. The table shows the distances Jerry roller skated.

   About how far did Jerry skate on Tuesday and Sunday?

Jerry's Roller Skating Distances	
Day	Distance (mi)
Tuesday	$3\frac{1}{5}$
Thursday	$6\frac{3}{7}$
Saturday	$8\frac{1}{7}$
Sunday	$2\frac{6}{7}$

Copyright © by Holt McDougal.
All rights reserved.

Holt McDougal Mathematics

4-1 Divisibility

Copy and complete the table. Write *yes* if the number is divisible by the given number. Write *no* if it is not.

	2	3	4	5	6	9	10
1. 459	no					yes	
2. 370	yes						
3. 1,366		no					
4. 13,950				yes			

Tell whether each statement is true or false. Explain your answer.

5. All even numbers are divisible by 4.

6. All numbers that are divisible by 10 are also divisible by 5.

7. There were 120 students that went a field trip. Kirby put them into small groups of less than 10 students, so that all groups had the same number of students. What were all the possible group sizes Kirby could have made?

4-2 Factors and Prime Factorization

Write each number as a product in two different ways.

8. 26

9. 70

10. 42

11. 96

Find the prime factorization of each number.

12. 88

13. 170

14. 306

15. 324

Copyright © by Holt McDougal.
All rights reserved.

Holt McDougal Mathematics

4-3 Greatest Common Factor

Write the GCF of each set of numbers.

16. 50 and 72

17. 14 and 35

18. 75, 115 and 150

19. 32, 80, and 108

20. 48, 120, and 144

21. $2^2 \cdot 5 \cdot 7^2$ and $2^3 \cdot 3^2 \cdot 5^2$

22. Jillian is making centerpieces for her parents' anniversary party. She has 48 tulips, 36 lilies and 12 roses. What is the greatest number of centerpieces she can make if each type of flower is distributed equally among the centerpieces?

4-4 Decimals and Fractions

Order the fractions and decimals from least to greatest.

23. $\frac{3}{8}$, 0.37, $\frac{1}{3}$

24. $\frac{5}{6}$, 0.91, $\frac{7}{8}$

25. $\frac{4}{9}$, 0.42, 0.90

Write each decimal in expanded form and use a whole number or fraction for each place value.

26. 0.64

27. 52.6

28. 17.31

29. 112.13

Write each fraction as a decimal. Tell whether the decimal terminates or repeats.

30. $\frac{3}{20}$

31. $\frac{5}{18}$

32. $\frac{11}{9}$

33. $\frac{3}{15}$

Compare. Write <, >, or =.

34. $\frac{2}{9}$ ▇ 0.29

35. 0.38 ▇ $\frac{3}{8}$

36. $\frac{4}{5}$ ▇ 0.80

Copyright © by Holt McDougal.
All rights reserved.

Holt McDougal Mathematics

4-5 Equivalent Fractions

Find missing numbers that make the fractions equivalent.

37. $\dfrac{1}{4} = \dfrac{6}{\blacksquare}$ **38.** $\dfrac{5}{8} = \dfrac{\blacksquare}{40}$ **39.** $\dfrac{3}{18} = \dfrac{1}{\blacksquare}$ **40.** $\dfrac{12}{16} = \dfrac{3}{\blacksquare}$

Find two equivalent fractions for each fraction.

41. $\dfrac{4}{15}$ **42.** $\dfrac{8}{10}$ **43.** $\dfrac{6}{8}$ **44.** $\dfrac{7}{21}$

Write two equivalent fractions represented by each picture.

45.

46.

4-6 Mixed Numbers and Improper Fractions

Write each mixed number as an improper fraction.

47. $8\dfrac{3}{7}$ **48.** $3\dfrac{7}{12}$ **49.** $12\dfrac{1}{9}$ **50.** $15\dfrac{2}{3}$

Write each improper fraction as a mixed number or whole number.

51. $\dfrac{32}{5}$ **52.** $\dfrac{16}{3}$ **53.** $\dfrac{42}{7}$ **54.** $\dfrac{85}{8}$

Replace each shape with a number that will make the equation correct.

55. $\blacksquare\dfrac{3}{10} = \dfrac{53}{\blacksquare}$ **56.** $\blacksquare\dfrac{3}{28} = \dfrac{171}{\blacksquare}$ **57.** $\blacksquare\dfrac{1}{16} = \dfrac{113}{\blacksquare}$

Write each improper fraction as a decimal. Then use <, >, or = to compare.

58. $\dfrac{14}{9}$ $\blacksquare$ 1.4 **59.** $\dfrac{64}{5}$ $\blacksquare$ 12.80 **60.** 7.27 $\blacksquare$ $\dfrac{58}{8}$

Copyright © by Holt McDougal.
All rights reserved.

Holt McDougal Mathematics

4-7 Comparing and Ordering Fractions

Compare. Write <, >, or =.

61. $\frac{5}{12}$ ■ $\frac{6}{10}$　　**62.** $\frac{2}{3}$ ■ $\frac{9}{14}$　　**63.** $\frac{4}{11}$ ■ $\frac{3}{7}$　　**64.** $\frac{11}{16}$ ■ $\frac{7}{19}$

Order the numbers from least to greatest.

65. $3\frac{1}{5}$, 3, $2\frac{7}{8}$, $2\frac{3}{8}$, $3\frac{4}{5}$　　　　**66.** $6\frac{3}{7}$, 6, $5\frac{4}{7}$, $6\frac{1}{4}$, $5\frac{4}{9}$

4-8 Adding and Subtracting with Like Denominators

Write each sum or difference in simplest form.

67. $\frac{3}{18} + \frac{5}{18}$　　**68.** $3\frac{21}{28} - \frac{7}{28}$　　**69.** $\frac{37}{75} + \frac{21}{75} + \frac{7}{75}$

Evaluate. Write each answer in simplest form.

70. $b + \frac{9}{16}$ for $b = \frac{3}{16}$　　　　**71.** $k - 4\frac{5}{28}$ for $k = 9\frac{27}{28}$

72. Rick had 5 cups of blueberries. He used $1\frac{3}{4}$ cups to make pancakes and $2\frac{1}{4}$ cups to make smoothies. How many cups of blueberries does Rick have now?

4-9 Estimating Fraction Sums and Differences

Estimate each sum or difference to compare. Write <, >, or =.

73. $3\frac{8}{9} + 4\frac{5}{12}$ ■ 8　　**74.** $8\frac{13}{15} - \frac{1}{12}$ ■ 9　　**75.** $4\frac{15}{16} + 1\frac{2}{13}$ ■ 7

Estimate.

76. $\frac{6}{17} + \frac{2}{13} + \frac{9}{11}$　　**77.** $8\frac{17}{19} - 3\frac{2}{15} - 1\frac{12}{13}$　　**78.** $12\frac{5}{12} + 14\frac{10}{13} + \frac{1}{9}$

Big Ideas

Answer these questions to summarize the important concepts from Chapter 4 in your own words.

1. Explain the difference between a prime number and a composite number.

2. List two methods that can be used to find the greatest common factor of a set of numbers.

3. Explain how to write a fraction as a decimal. Explain how to write a decimal as a fraction.

4. Explain how to change a mixed number to an improper fraction and how to change an improper fraction to a mixed number.

For more review of Chapter 4:

• Complete the Chapter 4 Study Guide and Review on pages 208–210 of your textbook.

• Complete the Ready to Go On quizzes on pages 172, 190, and 204 of your textbook.

Copyright © by Holt McDougal.
All rights reserved.

Holt McDougal Mathematics

Least Common Multiple

LESSON 5-1

Lesson Objectives

Find the least common multiple (LCM) of a group of numbers

Vocabulary

least common multiple (LCM) (p. 218) _____

_____

Additional Examples

Example 1

English muffins come in packs of 8, and eggs come in cartons of 12. If there are 24 students, what is the least number of packs and cartons needed so that each student has a muffin sandwich with one egg?

Draw muffins in groups of ☐ . Draw eggs in groups of ☐ . Stop when you have drawn the same number of each.

There are ☐ English muffins and ☐ eggs.

So ☐ packs of English muffins and ☐ cartons of eggs are needed.

Copyright © by Holt McDougal.
All rights reserved.

Holt McDougal Mathematics

Example 2

Find the least common multiple (LCM).

Method 1: Use a number line.

A. 3 and 4

Use a number line to skip count by ☐ and ☐ .

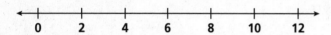

The least common multiple (LCM) of 3 and 4 is ☐ .

Method 2: Use a list.

B. 4, 5, and 8

List ☐ of 4, 5, and 8.

Find the ☐ number that is in all the lists.

4: 4, 8, 12, 16, 20, 24, 28, 32, 36, 40, 44, . . .

5: 5, 10, 15, 20, 25, 30, 35, 40, 45, . . .

8: 8, 16, 24, 32, 40, 48, . . .

LCM: ☐

Method 3: Use prime factorization.

C. 6 and 20

$6 = 2 \cdot 3$ Write the prime ☐ of each number.

$20 = 2 \cdot \quad 2 \cdot 5$ Line up the ☐ factors.

$2 \cdot 3 \cdot 2 \cdot 5$

$2 \cdot 3 \cdot 2 \cdot 5 = $ ☐   To find the LCM, multiply one number from each column.

Copyright © by Holt McDougal.
All rights reserved.

Holt McDougal Mathematics

Find the least common multiple (LCM).

Method 3: Use prime factorization.

 D. 15, 6, and 4

   15 =   3 · 5   Write the prime

                                  [   ]

                                  of each number in exponential form.

   6 = 2 · 3

   4 = 2^2

      $2^2 · 3 · 5$ To find the LCM, multiply each prime factor
                                  once with the greatest exponent used in any of
                                  the prime factorizations.

      $2^2 · 3 · 5 =$ [   ]

Check It Out!

1. Dog cookies come in packages of 6, and bones come in bags of 9. If
   there are 18 dogs, what is the least number of packages and bags
   needed so that each dog has a treat box with one bone and one
   cookie, and there are no bones or cookies left over?

   [   ]

2. Find the least common multiple of 3, 4, and 9.

   [   ]

Copyright © by Holt McDougal.
All rights reserved.

Holt McDougal Mathematics

Adding and Subtracting with Unlike Denominators

Lesson Objectives

Add and subtract fractions with unlike denominators

Vocabulary

least common denominator (LCD) (p. 224) _____

_____

Additional Examples

Example 1

Mark made a pizza with pepperoni covering $\frac{1}{4}$ of the pizza and onions covering another $\frac{1}{3}$. What fraction of the pizza is covered by pepperoni or onions?

Add $\frac{1}{4} + \frac{1}{3}$.

$\frac{1}{4}$

$+ \frac{1}{3}$

$\frac{1}{4} \rightarrow \boxed{}$ Find a $\boxed{}$ denominator for $\boxed{}$ and $\boxed{}$.

Write $\boxed{}$ fractions with $\boxed{}$ as the common denominator.

$+ \frac{1}{3} \rightarrow \boxed{}$ Add the $\boxed{}$. Keep the common denominator.

The pepperoni or onions cover $\boxed{}$ of the pizza.

Copyright © by Holt McDougal.
All rights reserved.

Holt McDougal Mathematics

Example 2

Add or subtract. Write each answer in simplest form.

Method 1: Multiplying denominators.

A. $\frac{7}{10} - \frac{3}{8}$

$\frac{7}{10} - \frac{3}{8}$ Multiply the denominators. ☐ · ☐ = ☐

☐ − ☐   Write ☐ fractions.

$\frac{26}{80}$ Subtract.

     Write the answer in simplest form.

Method 2: Use the LCD.

B. $\frac{11}{12} - \frac{3}{8}$

$\frac{11}{12} - \frac{3}{8}$ The LCD is ☐.

☐ − ☐   Write ☐ fractions.

     Subtract.

Method 3: Use mental math.

C. $\frac{5}{16} + \frac{1}{8}$

$\frac{5}{16} + \frac{1}{8}$ Think: ☐ is a multiple of ☐, so the LCD is ☐.

$\frac{5}{16} +$ ☐   Rewrite $\frac{1}{8}$ with a denominator of 16.

     Add.

Copyright © by Holt McDougal.
All rights reserved.

Holt McDougal Mathematics

D. $\frac{5}{16} - \frac{1}{8}$

$\frac{5}{16} - \frac{1}{8}$ Think: ☐ is a multiple of ☐, so the LCD is ☐.

$\frac{5}{16} -$ ☐   Rewrite $\frac{1}{8}$ with a denominator of 16.

☐   Subtract.

Check It Out!

1. Tori made a pizza with peppers covering $\frac{1}{3}$ and ham covering another $\frac{1}{2}$. What fraction of the pizza is covered by peppers and ham?

☐

2. Add or subtract. Write the answer in simplest form. $\frac{8}{10} - \frac{2}{6}$

☐

Copyright © by Holt McDougal.
All rights reserved.

Holt McDougal Mathematics

Adding and Subtracting Mixed Numbers

Lesson Objectives

Add and subtract mixed numbers with unlike denominators

Additional Examples

Example 1

Find each sum or difference. Write the answer in simplest form.

A. $3\frac{1}{8} + 1\frac{5}{6}$

$3\frac{1}{8} \longrightarrow 3\frac{6}{48}$

$+ 1\frac{5}{6} \longrightarrow + 1\frac{40}{48}$

$\boxed{} = \boxed{}$

Multiply the denominators. $8 \cdot 6 = 48$

Write $\boxed{}$ fractions with a denominator of 48.

Add the $\boxed{}$ and then $\boxed{}$ numbers, and simplify.

B. $5\frac{2}{3} - 1\frac{1}{4}$

$5\frac{2}{3} \longrightarrow \boxed{}$

$- 1\frac{1}{4} \longrightarrow - \boxed{}$

$\boxed{}$

The LCD of the denominators is 12.

Write $\boxed{}$ fractions with a denominator of 12.

Subtract the $\boxed{}$ and then the $\boxed{}$ numbers.

C. $2\frac{1}{2} + 4\frac{4}{5}$

$2\frac{1}{2} \longrightarrow \boxed{}$

$+ 4\frac{4}{5} \longrightarrow + \boxed{}$

$\boxed{} = \boxed{}$

The LCD of the denominators is 10.

Write $\boxed{}$ fractions with a denominator of 10.

Add the $\boxed{}$ and then the $\boxed{}$ numbers. $6\frac{13}{10} = 6 + 1\frac{3}{10}$

Copyright © by Holt McDougal.
All rights reserved.

Holt McDougal Mathematics

Example 2

The length of Jen's kitten's body is $10\frac{1}{4}$ inches. Its tail is $5\frac{1}{8}$ inches long. What is the total length of its body and tail?

Add $10\frac{1}{4} + 5\frac{1}{8}$.

$10\frac{1}{4} \rightarrow$ [ ]   Find a [ ] denominator. Write

[ ] fractions with the LCD,

[ ] , as the denominator.

$+ 5\frac{1}{8} \rightarrow + 5\frac{1}{8}$

[ ]

Add the [ ] and then

[ ] numbers.

The total length of the kitten's body and tail is [ ] inches.

Check It Out!

1. Find the sum. Write the answer in simplest form.

$2\frac{7}{8} + 4\frac{2}{3}$

2. The length of Regina's mouse's body is $2\frac{2}{3}$ inches. Its tail is $2\frac{1}{6}$ inches long. What is the total length of its body and tail?

Copyright © by Holt McDougal.
All rights reserved.

Holt McDougal Mathematics

Regrouping to Subtract Mixed Numbers

Lesson Objectives

Regroup mixed numbers to subtract

Additional Examples

Example 1

Subtract. Write each answer in simplest form.

A. $6 - 3\frac{2}{3}$

$6 \rightarrow \boxed{}$

$\begin{array}{r} -3\frac{2}{3} \rightarrow -3\frac{2}{3} \\ \hline \boxed{} \end{array}$

Write 6 as a $\boxed{}$ number with a denominator of $\boxed{}$.

Rename 6 as $5 + \frac{3}{3}$.

Subtract the $\boxed{}$ and then the $\boxed{}$ numbers.

B. $5\frac{1}{3} - 2\frac{3}{4}$

$\boxed{}$

$5\frac{1}{3} \rightarrow \boxed{}$

$2\frac{3}{4} \rightarrow \boxed{}$

$5\frac{4}{12} \rightarrow \boxed{}$

$\begin{array}{r} -2\frac{9}{12} \rightarrow \boxed{} \\ \hline \end{array}$

$\boxed{}$

Estimate the difference.

$\boxed{}$ is a multiple of 3 and 4, so $\boxed{}$ is a common denominator.

Regroup $5\frac{4}{12}$ as $4 + \boxed{} = 4 + \boxed{} + \boxed{}$

Subtract the $\boxed{}$ and then the $\boxed{}$ numbers.

Copyright © by Holt McDougal.
All rights reserved.

Holt McDougal Mathematics

Example 2

Li is making a quilt. She needs 15 yards of fabric.

A. Li has $2\frac{3}{4}$ yards of fabric. How many more yards does she need?

$15 \longrightarrow$ [ ]   Write 15 as a [ ] number with a

denominator of [ ].

$-2\frac{3}{4} \longrightarrow -2\frac{3}{4}$ Rename 15 as 14 + [ ].

[ ]   Subtract the [ ] and then the

[ ] numbers.

Li needs another [ ] yards of fabric.

B. If Li uses $11\frac{1}{6}$ yards of fabric, how much of the 15 yards will she have left?

$15 \longrightarrow$ [ ]   Write 15 as a [ ] number with a

denominator of [ ].

$-11\frac{1}{6} \longrightarrow -11\frac{1}{6}$ Rename 15 as 14 + [ ].

[ ]   Subtract the [ ] and then the

[ ] numbers.

Li will have [ ] yards of fabric left.

Check It Out!

1. Subtract. Write the answer in simplest form.

$7\frac{1}{6} - 3\frac{7}{12}$

2. Peggy is making curtains. She needs 13 yards of fabric. Peggy has $4\frac{5}{6}$ yards of fabric. How many more yards does she need?

Copyright © by Holt McDougal.
All rights reserved.

Holt McDougal Mathematics

Solving Fraction Equations: Addition and Subtraction

Lesson Objectives

Solve equations by adding and subtracting fractions

Additional Examples

Example 1

Solve each equation. Write the solution in simplest form.

A. $x + 5\frac{3}{5} = 14$

$\quad -5\frac{3}{5} \qquad -5\frac{3}{5}$ Subtract ⬚ from both sides to undo the ⬚.

$\quad x = \boxed{} - 5\frac{3}{5}$ Rename 14 as ⬚.

$\quad x = \boxed{}$ Subtract.

B. $3\frac{2}{9} = x - 4\frac{1}{3}$

$\quad +4\frac{1}{3} \qquad +4\frac{1}{3}$ Add ⬚ to both sides to undo the ⬚.

$\quad 3\frac{2}{9} + \boxed{} = x$ Find a ⬚ denominator.

$\quad \boxed{} = x$ Add.

C. $6\frac{1}{6} = m + \frac{7}{12}$

$\quad -\frac{7}{12} \qquad -\frac{7}{12}$ Subtract ⬚ from both sides to undo the ⬚.

$\quad 6\frac{2}{12} - \frac{7}{12} = m$ Find a ⬚ denominator.

$\quad \boxed{} - \frac{7}{12} = m$ Rename $6\frac{2}{12}$ as $\boxed{} + \frac{2}{12}$.

$\quad \boxed{} = m$ Subtract.

Copyright © by Holt McDougal.
All rights reserved.

Holt McDougal Mathematics

D. $w - \frac{4}{5} = 3\frac{3}{10}$

$+ \frac{4}{5} \quad + \frac{4}{5}$ Add $\boxed{}$ to both sides to undo the $\boxed{}$.

$3\frac{3}{10} + \boxed{}$ Find a common denominator.

$\boxed{} = \boxed{} = w$ Add and rename $\boxed{}$ as $\boxed{} + \boxed{}$.

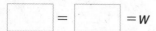

Example 2

Linda's dog weighs $85\frac{1}{4}$ pounds. If Linda's dog weighs $17\frac{1}{2}$ pounds less than Ian's dog, how much does Ian's dog weigh?

$d - 17\frac{1}{2} = \quad 85\frac{1}{4}$ Let d represent the weight of Ian's dog.

$+ \boxed{} \quad + \boxed{}$ Add $\boxed{}$ to both sides to undo the $\boxed{}$.

$d = \boxed{}$

Ian's dog weighs $\boxed{}$ pounds.

Check It Out!

1. Solve the equation. Write the solution in simplest form.

$5\frac{2}{5} = m + \frac{7}{10}$

2. Jimmy's cat weighs $13\frac{2}{3}$ pounds. If Jimmy's cat weighs $4\frac{1}{6}$ pounds less than Vicki's cat, how much does Vicki's cat weigh?

Copyright © by Holt McDougal.
All rights reserved.

Holt McDougal Mathematics

Multiplying Fractions by Whole Numbers

Lesson Objectives

Multiply fractions by whole numbers

Additional Examples

Example 1

Multiply. Write each answer in simplest form.

A. $7 \cdot \frac{1}{9}$

$7 \cdot \frac{1}{9} = \frac{7 \cdot 1}{1 \cdot 9}$ Write 7 as a ⬜. Multiply

⬜ and ⬜.

$=$ ⬜

B. $6 \cdot \frac{1}{8}$

$6 \cdot \frac{1}{8} = \frac{6 \cdot 1}{1 \cdot 8}$ Write 6 as a ⬜. Multiply

⬜ and ⬜.

$=$ ⬜

$=$ ⬜   Write your answer in simplest form.

C. $8 \cdot \frac{2}{3}$

$8 \cdot \frac{2}{3} = \frac{8 \cdot 2}{1 \cdot 3}$ Write 8 as a ⬜. Multiply

⬜ and

⬜.

$=$ ⬜ , or ⬜

Copyright © by Holt McDougal.
All rights reserved.

Holt McDougal Mathematics

Example 2

Evaluate 4x for each value of x. Write each answer in simplest form.

A. $x = \dfrac{1}{10}$

$4x$	Write the expression.
$4 \cdot \boxed{}$	Substitute $\boxed{}$ for x.
$\boxed{} \cdot \dfrac{1}{10} = \boxed{}$	Multiply.
$= \boxed{}$	Write your answer in simplest form.

B. $x = \dfrac{3}{8}$

$4x$	Write the expression.
$4 \cdot \boxed{}$	Substitute $\boxed{}$ for x.
$\boxed{} \cdot \dfrac{3}{8} = \dfrac{12}{8}$	Multiply.
$= \boxed{}$ or $\boxed{}$	Write your answer in simplest form.

Example 3

There are 25 students in the music club. Of those students, $\dfrac{3}{5}$ are also in the band. How many music club students are in the band?

To find $\dfrac{3}{5}$ of 25, multiply.

$$\dfrac{3}{5} \cdot 25 = \dfrac{3}{5} \cdot \boxed{}$$

$$= \dfrac{\boxed{}}{5} \qquad \text{Divide } \boxed{} \text{ by 5 and write your answer in simplest form.}$$

$$= \boxed{}$$

There are $\boxed{}$ music club students in the band.

Copyright © by Holt McDougal.
All rights reserved.

Holt McDougal Mathematics

Check It Out!

1. Multiply. Write the answer in simplest form.

   $9 \cdot \dfrac{3}{4}$

2. Evaluate $3x$ for the value of x. Write the answer in simplest form.

   $x = \dfrac{1}{9}$

3. There are 50 people on the football team. Of those people, $\dfrac{1}{5}$ are also on the basketball team. How many people on the football team are also on the basketball team?

Copyright © by Holt McDougal.
All rights reserved.

Holt McDougal Mathematics

Multiplying Fractions

Lesson Objectives

Multiply fractions

Additional Examples

Multiply. Write each answer in simplest form.

A. $\frac{1}{4} \cdot \frac{2}{5}$

$\frac{1}{4} \cdot \frac{2}{5} = \frac{1 \cdot 2}{4 \cdot 5}$ Multiply [   ]. Multiply

[   ].

= [   ]   The GCF of 2 and 20 is [   ].

= [   ]   The answer is in simplest form.

B. $\frac{5}{7} \cdot \frac{4}{15}$

$\overset{1}{\cancel{5}}{7} \cdot \frac{4}{\underset{3}{\cancel{15}}} = \frac{1}{7} \cdot \frac{4}{3}$ Use the GCF to simplify the fractions before

[   ]. The greatest common

factor of 5 and 15 is [   ].

$= \frac{1 \cdot 4}{7 \cdot 3}$ Multiply [   ]. Multiply

[   ].

= [   ]   The answer is in simplest form.

C. $\frac{4}{9} \cdot \frac{6}{10}$

$\frac{4}{9} \cdot \frac{6}{10} = \frac{4 \cdot 6}{9 \cdot 10}$ Multiply [   ]. Multiply [   ].

= [   ]   The GCF of [   ] and [   ] is [   ].

= [   ]   The answer is in simplest form.

Copyright © by Holt McDougal.
All rights reserved.

Holt McDougal Mathematics

Example 2

Evaluate the expression $b \cdot \frac{2}{5}$ for each value of b. Write the answer in simplest form.

A. $b = \frac{1}{3}$

$b \cdot \frac{2}{5}$

$\boxed{} \cdot \frac{2}{5}$ Substitute $\boxed{}$ for b.

$\frac{1 \cdot 2}{3 \cdot 5}$ Multiply.

$\boxed{}$ The answer is in simplest form.

B. $b = \frac{3}{8}$ $b \cdot \frac{2}{5}$

$\boxed{} \cdot \frac{2}{5}$ Substitute $\boxed{}$ for b.

$\frac{3}{{}_4 \cancel{8}} \cdot \frac{\cancel{2}^1}{5}$ Use the $\boxed{}$ to simplify.

$\frac{3 \cdot 1}{4 \cdot 5}$ Multiply.

$\boxed{}$ The answer is in simplest form.

Check It Out!

1. Multiply. Write the answer in simplest form.

$\frac{3}{7} \cdot \frac{5}{9}$

2. Evaluate the expression $c \cdot \frac{1}{4}$ for the value of c. Write the answer in simplest form.

$c = \frac{1}{7}$

Copyright © by Holt McDougal.
All rights reserved.

Holt McDougal Mathematics

Multiplying Mixed Numbers

Lesson Objectives

Multiply mixed numbers

Additional Examples

Example 1

Multiply. Write each answer in simplest form.

A. $\frac{1}{4} \cdot 1\frac{1}{3}$

$\frac{1}{4} \cdot \boxed{}$ Write $1\frac{1}{3}$ as an improper fraction. $1\frac{1}{3} = \boxed{}$

$\frac{1 \cdot 4}{4 \cdot 3}$ Multiply $\boxed{}$. Multiply

$\boxed{}$ $\boxed{}$.

$\boxed{}$ Write the answer in simplest form.

B. $3\frac{1}{2} \cdot \frac{4}{5}$

$\boxed{} \cdot \frac{4}{5}$ Write $3\frac{1}{2}$ as an improper fraction. $3\frac{1}{2} = \boxed{}$

$\frac{7 \cdot 4}{2 \cdot 5}$ Multiply $\boxed{}$. Multiply

$\boxed{}$.

$\boxed{}$ Write the answer in simplest form.

$\boxed{} = \boxed{}$ You can write the anwer as a mixed number.

C. $\frac{12}{13} \cdot 2\frac{3}{8}$

$\frac{12}{13} \cdot \boxed{}$ Write $2\frac{3}{8}$ as an improper fraction. $2\frac{3}{8} = \boxed{}$

$\frac{\overset{3}{\cancel{12}}}{13} \cdot \frac{19}{\underset{2}{\cancel{8}}}$ Use the GCF to simplify before

$\boxed{}$.

$\frac{3 \cdot 19}{13 \cdot 2}$

$\boxed{} = \boxed{}$ You can write the anwer as a mixed number.

Copyright © by Holt McDougal.
All rights reserved.

Holt McDougal Mathematics

Example 2

Find each product. Write the answer in simplest form.

A. $1\frac{2}{3} \cdot 2\frac{1}{7}$

$\boxed{} \cdot \boxed{}$ Write the mixed numbers as improper fractions.

$1\frac{2}{3} = \boxed{}$ $2\frac{1}{7} = \boxed{}$

$\dfrac{5 \cdot 15}{3 \cdot 7}$ Multiply $\boxed{}$. Multiply
$\boxed{}$.

$\boxed{} = \boxed{}$ You can write the improper fraction as a mixed
number.
Simplify.

B. $1\frac{3}{8} \cdot 2\frac{2}{5}$

$\boxed{} \cdot \boxed{}$ Write the mixed numbers as improper fractions.

$1\frac{3}{8} = \boxed{}$ $2\frac{2}{5} = \boxed{}$

$\dfrac{11}{\cancel{8}_2} \cdot \dfrac{\cancel{12}^{3}}{5}$ Use the GCF to simplify before
$\boxed{}$.

$\dfrac{11 \cdot 3}{2 \cdot 5}$ Multiply $\boxed{}$. Multiply
$\boxed{}$.

$\boxed{} = \boxed{}$ Simplify.

Check It Out!

1. Multiply. Write the answer in simplest form.

$2\frac{2}{3} \cdot \frac{5}{6} = \boxed{}$

2. Find the product. Write the answer in simplest form.

$1\frac{3}{4} \cdot 2\frac{1}{6} = \boxed{}$

Copyright © by Holt McDougal.
All rights reserved.

Holt McDougal Mathematics

Dividing Fractions and Mixed Numbers

Lesson Objectives

Divide fractions and mixed numbers

Vocabulary

reciprocal (p. 260) _____

_____

multiplicative inverse (p. 260) _____

_____

Additional Examples

Example 1

Find the reciprocal.

A. $\frac{1}{9}$

$\frac{1}{9} \cdot \blacksquare = 1$ Think: $\frac{1}{9}$ of what number is 1?

$\frac{1}{9} \cdot \boxed{} = 1$ $\frac{1}{9}$ of $\boxed{}$ is 1.

The reciprocal of $\frac{1}{9}$ is $\boxed{}$.

B. $\frac{2}{3}$

$\frac{2}{3} \cdot \blacksquare = 1$ Think: $\frac{2}{3}$ of what number is 1?

$\frac{2}{3} \cdot \boxed{} = 1$ $\frac{2}{3}$ of $\boxed{}$ is 1.

The reciprocal of $\frac{2}{3}$ is $\boxed{}$.

C. $3\frac{1}{5}$

$\frac{16}{5} \cdot \blacksquare = 1$ Write $3\frac{1}{5}$ as $\frac{16}{5}$.

$\frac{16}{5} \cdot \boxed{} = \frac{80}{80} = 1$ $\frac{16}{5}$ of $\boxed{}$ is 1.

The reciprocal of $\frac{16}{5}$ is $\boxed{}$.

Copyright © by Holt McDougal.
All rights reserved.

Holt McDougal Mathematics

Example 2

Divide. Write each answer in simplest form.

A. $\frac{8}{7} \div 7$

$\frac{8}{7} \div 7 = \frac{8}{7} \cdot \boxed{}$ Rewrite as multiplication using the reciprocal of 7, $\boxed{}$.

$= \frac{8 \cdot 1}{7 \cdot 7}$ Multiply by the reciprocal.

$= \boxed{}$ The answer is in simplest form.

B. $\frac{5}{6} \div \frac{2}{3}$

$\frac{5}{6} \div \frac{2}{3} = \frac{5}{6} \cdot \boxed{}$ Rewrite as multiplication using the reciprocal of $\frac{2}{3}$, $\boxed{}$.

$= \frac{5 \cdot \cancel{3}^{1}}{_{2}\cancel{6} \cdot 2}$ Simplify before $\boxed{}$.

$= \boxed{}$ Multiply.

$= \boxed{}$ You can write the answer as a mixed number.

Check It Out!

1. Find the reciprocal.

$4\frac{1}{8}$

2. Divide. Write the answer in simplest form.

$\frac{7}{10} \div \frac{1}{5}$

Copyright © by Holt McDougal.
All rights reserved.

Holt McDougal Mathematics

Solving Fraction Equations: Multiplication and Division

Lesson Objectives

Solve equations by multiplying and dividing fractions

Additional Examples

Example 1

Solve each equation. Write the answer in simplest form.

A. $\frac{3}{5}j = 25$

$\frac{3}{5}j \div \boxed{} = 25 \div \boxed{}$ $\boxed{}$ both sides of the equation by $\boxed{}$.

$\frac{3}{5}j \cdot \frac{5}{3} = 25 \cdot \frac{5}{3}$ Multiply by $\boxed{}$, the reciprocal of $\boxed{}$.

$j = 25 \cdot \frac{5}{3}$

$j = \frac{25 \cdot 5}{1 \cdot 3}$

$j = \boxed{}$, or $\boxed{}$

B. $7x = \frac{2}{5}$

$\frac{7x}{1} \cdot \boxed{} = \frac{2}{5} \cdot \boxed{}$ Multiply both sides by the $\boxed{}$ of 7.

$x = \frac{2 \cdot 1}{5 \cdot 7}$

$x = \boxed{}$ The answer is in simplest form.

C. $\frac{5y}{8} = 6$

$\frac{5y}{8} \div \boxed{} = \frac{6}{1} \div \boxed{}$ Divide both sides by $\boxed{}$.

$\frac{5y}{8} \cdot \boxed{} = \frac{6}{1} \cdot \boxed{}$ Multiply by the reciprocal of $\boxed{}$.

$y = \boxed{}$ or $\boxed{}$

Copyright © by Holt McDougal.
All rights reserved.

Holt McDougal Mathematics

Example 2 **PROBLEM SOLVING APPLICATION**

Dexter makes $\frac{2}{3}$ of a recipe, and he uses 12 cups of powdered milk. How many cups of powdered milk are in the recipe?

1. **Understand the Problem**

   The answer will be the number of cups of powdered milk in the recipe. List the important information:

   • He makes ☐ of the recipe.   • He uses ☐ cups of powdered milk.

2. **Make a Plan**

   Write and solve an equation. Let x represent the number of cups in the recipe. He uses 12 cups, which is two-thirds of the amount in the recipe. $12 = \frac{2}{3}x$

3. **Solve**

   $$12 = \frac{2}{3}x$$

   $12 \cdot \boxed{} = \frac{2}{3}x \cdot \boxed{}$ Multiply both sides by ☐, the reciprocal of $\frac{2}{3}$.

   $\overset{6}{\cancel{12}} \cdot \dfrac{3}{\underset{1}{\cancel{2}}} = x$ Simplify. Then multiply.

   ☐ $= x$

   There are ☐ cups of powdered milk in the recipe.

4. **Look Back**

   Check $12 \overset{?}{=} \frac{2}{3}(18)$ Substitute 18 for x.

   $12 \overset{?}{=} \dfrac{\overset{12}{\cancel{36}}}{\cancel{3}}$ Multiply and simplify.

   $12 \overset{?}{=} 12$ ✓   18 is the solution.

Check It Out!

1. Solve the equation. Write the answer in simplest form.

   $\frac{3}{4}j = 19$ ▮

2. Rich makes $\frac{2}{5}$ of a recipe, and he uses 8 cups of wheat flour. How many

   cups of wheat flour are in the recipe?

Copyright © by Holt McDougal.
All rights reserved.
Holt McDougal Mathematics

5-1 Least Common Multiple

1. What is the LCM of 8 and 16?

3. What is the LCM of 5, 8 and 12?

2. What is the LCM of 9 and 13?

4. What is the LCM of 2, 5, 6, and 8?

Find a pair of numbers that has the given characteristics.

5. The LCM of two numbers is 60. The sum of the numbers is 32.

6. The LCM of two numbers is 56. The difference of the numbers is 6.

7. Pencils come in packs of 10, and pens come in packs of 8. If there are 40 students, what is the least number of packs of pencils and pens needed so that each student gets one pencil and one pen and there are none left over?

5-2 Adding and Subtracting with Unlike Denominators

Find each sum or difference. Write your answer in simplest form.

8. $\frac{3}{10} + \frac{5}{8}$

9. $\frac{1}{3} - \frac{1}{4}$

10. $\frac{3}{8} + \frac{1}{3}$

11. $\frac{5}{11} - \frac{2}{7}$

Evaluate each expression for $c = \frac{2}{3}$. Write your answer in simplest form.

12. $c + \frac{1}{8}$

13. $c - \frac{2}{7}$

14. $\frac{2}{9} + c$

15. $\frac{7}{10} - c$

Evaluate. Write each answer in simplest form.

16. $\frac{1}{5} + \frac{1}{10} + \frac{2}{5}$

17. $\frac{5}{12} - \frac{1}{6} + \frac{2}{3}$

18. $\frac{7}{8} - \frac{1}{2} + \frac{1}{4}$

19. $\frac{5}{14} - \frac{4}{28} + \frac{3}{7}$

20. Tina and her friends ate $\frac{2}{3}$ of a cake. Then Mike ate $\frac{1}{5}$ of the cake. What fraction of the cake was left?

5-3 Adding and Subtracting Mixed Numbers

Add or subtract. Write each answer in simplest form.

21. $12\frac{3}{5} + 16\frac{6}{10}$ **22.** $18\frac{5}{8} - 4\frac{1}{4}$ **23.** $20\frac{5}{9} + 14\frac{5}{12}$ **24.** $48\frac{4}{11} - 16\frac{1}{6}$

Evaluate each expression for $n = 2\frac{1}{4}$. **Write your answer in simplest form.**

25. $3\frac{3}{4} + n$ **26.** $7(5\frac{3}{8} + n)$ **27.** $n - 1\frac{3}{16}$ **28.** $5(4\frac{2}{3} - n)$

29. Kellie had a piece of wood trim $4\frac{2}{3}$ yards long. She cut the wood into two pieces. One piece of the wood trim was $3\frac{1}{2}$ yards long. How long was the other piece of wood trim?

5-4 Regrouping to Subtract Mixed Numbers

Find each difference. Write the answer in simplest form.

30. $11 - 5\frac{5}{7}$ **31.** $15\frac{2}{9} - 10\frac{2}{3}$ **32.** $19\frac{1}{6} - 6\frac{1}{3}$ **33.** $24\frac{2}{5} - 7\frac{3}{4}$

34. Jack used $4\frac{5}{8}$ pounds of a 30-pound bag of dog food to feed his dogs. How many pounds of dog food were left?

35. Felecia had a piece of ribbon that was $50\frac{1}{4}$ feet long. She used $15\frac{2}{3}$ feet for a project. How many feet were left on the original piece of ribbon?

36. At the start of the month, the snowfall total for the year was $18\frac{1}{8}$ inches. At the end of the month, the snowfall total for the year was 21 inches. How many inches of snow fell during the month?

Copyright © by Holt McDougal.
All rights reserved.

Holt McDougal Mathematics

5-5 Solving Fraction Equations: Addition and Subtraction

Find the solution to each equation. Check your answers.

37. $p + 4\frac{3}{4} = 9$　　　　**38.** $n - 5\frac{2}{5} = 2\frac{3}{10} + 1\frac{1}{5}$　　**39.** $12 - 3\frac{5}{8} = z - 2\frac{3}{8}$

40. Jenna built a card tower $9\frac{1}{2}$ inches taller than Callie's card tower. Callie's tower was $20\frac{1}{2}$ inches tall. How tall was Jenna's tower?

5-6 Multiplying Fractions by Whole Numbers

Evaluate each expression. Write each answer in simplest form.

41. $16y$ for $y = \frac{11}{16}$　**42.** $\frac{3}{4}b$ for $b = 28$　**43.** $\frac{1}{8}k$ for $k = 32$　**44.** $\frac{11}{20}p$ for $p = 80$

Compare. Write <, >, or =.

45. $2 \cdot \frac{4}{11}$ ■ $\frac{8}{11}$　　　　**46.** $5 \cdot \frac{3}{4}$ ■ $\frac{13}{15}$　　　　**47.** $2 \cdot \frac{5}{8}$ ■ $8 \cdot \frac{2}{5}$

5-7 Multiplying Fractions

Find each product. Simplify the answer.

48. $\frac{4}{5} \cdot \frac{3}{16}$　　　　　**49.** $\frac{9}{10} \cdot \frac{5}{8}$　　　　　**50.** $\frac{6}{7} \cdot \frac{1}{2} \cdot \frac{3}{5}$

Compare. Write <, >, or =.

51. $\frac{3}{7} \cdot \frac{2}{9}$ ■ $\frac{2}{3} \cdot \frac{9}{11}$　　**52.** $\frac{2}{3} \cdot \frac{4}{10}$ ■ $\frac{8}{15} \cdot \frac{1}{2}$　　**53.** $\frac{5}{6} \cdot \frac{1}{4}$ ■ $\frac{4}{5} \cdot \frac{3}{5}$

54. A recipe calls for $\frac{2}{3}$ cup of sugar. Eric wants to make $\frac{1}{2}$ of the recipe. What fraction of a cup of sugar will he need?

Copyright © by Holt McDougal.
All rights reserved.
Holt McDougal Mathematics

5-8 Multiplying Mixed Numbers

Write each product in simplest form.

55. $2\frac{1}{4} \cdot \frac{2}{9}$ **56.** $6 \cdot \frac{3}{5}$ **57.** $3\frac{1}{8} \cdot 2\frac{2}{3}$ **58.** $1\frac{9}{10} \cdot 5 \cdot \frac{4}{7}$

59. Sydney worked on her scrapbook project for $4\frac{4}{5}$ hours. She spent $\frac{1}{5}$ of that time journaling in the scrapbook. How much time did she spend journaling?

5-9 Dividing Fractions and Mixed Numbers

Decide whether the fractions in each pair are reciprocals. If not, write the reciprocal of each fraction.

60. $\frac{1}{8}$, 8   **61.** $\frac{5}{6}, \frac{18}{15}$ **62.** $\frac{4}{7}, \frac{21}{15}$ **63.** $\frac{4}{9}, \frac{8}{27}$

64. At Freezy Treats a jumbo serving of ice cream is $2\frac{3}{4}$ cups. A container holds 55 cups of ice cream. How many jumbo servings of ice cream are in the container?

5-10 Solving Fraction Equations: Multiplication and Division

Solve each equation. Write the answer in simplest form.

65. $3y = \frac{4}{5}$ **66.** $\frac{1}{8}w = 1\frac{3}{4}$ **67.** $9 = \frac{5a}{6}$ **68.** $8c = \frac{3}{7} \div \frac{2}{7}$

69. Elizabeth is planting flowers in window boxes. Each window box holds $3\frac{1}{3}$ pounds of dirt. Elizabeth has a 20-pound bag of dirt. How many window boxes can she fill with dirt?

Copyright © by Holt McDougal.
All rights reserved.

Holt McDougal Mathematics

Answer these question to summarize the important concepts from Chapter 5 in your own words.

1. How do you write the prime factorization of a number?

2. Explain how to add or subtract fractions with unlike denominators using the least common denominator (LCD).

3. Explain how to subtract $4\frac{5}{7}$ from 6.

4. Explain how to divide $4\frac{3}{4}$ by $2\frac{1}{2}$.

For more review of Chapter 5:

- Complete the Chapter 5 Study Guide and Review on pages 272–274 of your textbook.

- Complete the Ready to Go On quizzes on pages 242 and 268 of your textbook.

Copyright © by Holt McDougal.
All rights reserved.

Making a Table

Lesson Objectives

Use tables to record and organize data

Additional Examples

Example 1

Use the audience data to make a table. Then use your table to describe how attendance changed over time.

On May 1, there were 275 people in the audience at the school play. On May 2, there were 302 people. On May 3, there were 322 people.

Date	People in Audience

Make a table. Write the ☐ in

order so that you can see how the

attendance changed over time.

From the table you can see that the number of people in the audience

☐ from May 1 to May 3.

Example 2

Use the temperature data to make a table. Then use your table to find a pattern in the data and draw a conclusion.

At 3 A.M., the temperature was 53°F. At 5 A.M., it was 52°F. At 7 A.M., it was 50°F. At 9 A.M., it was 53°F. At 11 A.M., it was 57°F.

Time	Temperature (°F)

The temperature dropped until ☐,

then it rose. One conclusion is that the

☐ temperature on this day was 50°F.

Copyright © by Holt McDougal.
All rights reserved.

Holt McDougal Mathematics

Check It Out!

1. **Use the audience data to make a table. Then use your table to describe how attendance has changed over time.**

   On April 1, there were 212 people at the symphony. On May 1, there were 189 people. On June 1, there were 172 people.

   The number of people in the audience _____ from April 1 to June 1.

2. **Use the temperature data to make a table. Then use your table to find a pattern in the data and draw a conclusion.**

   At 2 A.M., the temperature was 48°F. At 4 A.M., it was 46°F. At 6 A.M., it was 44°F. At 8 A.M., it was 47°F. At 10 A.M., it was 51°F.

   The temperature dropped until _____, then it rose. One conclusion is that the _____ temperature on this day was 44°F.

Copyright © by Holt McDougal.
All rights reserved.

Holt McDougal Mathematics

Mean, Median, Mode and Range

Lesson Objectives

Find the mean, median, mode, and range of a data set

Vocabulary

mean (p. 288) _____

_____

median (p. 289) _____

_____

mode (p. 289) _____

_____

range (p. 289) _____

_____

Additional Examples

Example 1

Find the mean of each data set.

A.

Depth of Puddles (in.)						
5	8	3	5	4	2	1

Start by writing the data in numerical order. [   ]

mean: $1 + 2 + 3 + 4 + 5 + 5 + 8 =$ [   ] [   ] all values.

$28 \div$ [   ] $=$ [   ] [   ] the sum by

the [   ] of items.

The mean is [   ] inches.

Copyright © by Holt McDougal.
All rights reserved.

Holt McDougal Mathematics

Find the mean of each data set.

B.

Number of Points Scores			
96	75	84	7

Start by writing the data in numerical order. ☐

mean: $7 + 75 + 84 + 96 =$ ☐   ☐ all values.

$262 \div$ ☐ $=$ ☐   ☐ the sum by the

☐ of items.

The mean is ☐ points.

Example 2

Find the mean, median, mode, and range of the data set.

Car Wash Totals			
6th grade	12	7th grade	11
8th grade	14	9th grade	15

mean: $\dfrac{12 + 11 + 14 + 15}{4} =$ ☐

Write the data in numerical order: ☐

median: 11, (12, 13,) 15   There are an even number of items, so find

$\dfrac{12 + 13}{2} =$ ☐   the ☐ of the two middle values.

mode: ☐

range: $15 - 11 =$ ☐

The mean is ☐ ; the median is ☐ ; there is ☐ mode, and

the range is ☐ .

Copyright © by Holt McDougal.
All rights reserved.

Holt McDougal Mathematics

Check It Out!

1. Find the mean of the data set.

Rainfall per Month (in.)						
1	2	10	2	5	6	9

2. Find the mean, median, mode, and range of the data set.

Number of Vacation Days			
53	26	47	12

Copyright © by Holt McDougal.
All rights reserved.

Holt McDougal Mathematics

Additional Data and Outliers

Lesson Objectives

Learn the effect of additional data and outliers

Vocabulary

outlier (p. 292) _____

Additional Examples

Example 1

A. Find the mean, median, and mode of the data in the table.

EMS Football Games Won				
Year	1998	1999	2000	2001	2002
Games	11	5	7	5	7

mean = [ ]   modes = [ ]   median = [ ]

B. EMS also won 13 games in 1997 and 8 games in 1996. Add this data to the data in the table and find the mean, median, and mode.

mean = [ ]   modes = [ ]   median = [ ]

The [   ] increased by 1, the [   ] remained the same, and

the [   ] remained the same.

Example 2

Ms. Gray is 25 years old. She took a class with students who were 55, 52, 59, 61, 63, and 58 years old. Find the mean, median, and mode with and without Ms. Gray's age.

Data with Ms. Gray's age: mean ≈ ☐   ☐ mode

median = ☐

Data without Ms. Gray's age: mean = ☐   ☐ mode

median = ☐

When you add Ms. Gray's age, the mean decreases by about 4.7,

the ☐ stays the same, and the ☐ decreases by 0.5.

The ☐ is the most affected by the ☐. The median

is closer to most of the students' ages.

Example 3

The Yorks found 8 pairs of skates with the following prices:

   $35, $42, $75, $40, $47, $34, $45, $40

What are the mean, median, and mode of this data set? Which statistic best describes the data set?

mean = ☐   modes = ☐   median = ☐

The ☐ price is the best description of the prices. Most of the

skates cost about $ ☐ . The ☐ is higher than most of the

prices because of the $ ☐ skates.

Copyright © by Holt McDougal.
All rights reserved.

Holt McDougal Mathematics

Check It Out!

1. Find the mean, median, and mode of the data in the table.

MA Basketball Games Won					
Year	1998	1999	2000	2001	2002
Games	13	6	4	6	11

2. Ms. Pink is 56 years old. She volunteered to work with people who were 25, 22, 27, 24, 26, and 23 years old. Find the mean, median, and mode with and without Ms. Pink's age.

3. The Oswalds found 8 pairs of gloves with the following prices: $17, $15, $39, $12, $13, $16, $19, $15. What are the mean, median, and mode of this data set? Which statistic best describes the data set?

Copyright © by Holt McDougal.
All rights reserved.

Holt McDougal Mathematics

Bar Graphs

Lesson Objectives

Display and analyze data in bar graphs

Vocabulary

bar graph (p. 298) _____

_____

double-bar graph (p. 299) _____

_____

Additional Examples

Example 1

Use the bar graph to answer each question.

A. Which biome in the graph has the lowest average summer temperature?

Find the [_____] bar.

The [_____]

has the [_____] average summer

temperature.

B. Which biomes in the graph have an average summer temperature of 30°C or greater?

Find the bar or bars whose heights measure [____] or more than [____].

The [_____] and the [_____] have average

summer temperatures of 30°C or greater.

Average Summer Temperature

Temperature (°C): 40, 35, 30, 25, 20, 15, 10, 5, 0

Biomes: Deciduous forest, Rain forest, Grassland, Coniferous forest

Copyright © by Holt McDougal.
All rights reserved.

Holt McDougal Mathematics

Example 2

Use the data to make a bar graph.

Magazine Subscriptions Sold		
Grade 6	Grade 7	Grade 8
258	597	374

Step 1: Find an appropriate [   ]

and [   ]. The scale must include all of the data

[   ]. The interval separates the scale into [   ]

parts.

Step 2: Use the [   ] to determine the lengths

of the bars. Draw bars of equal [   ].

The bars cannot touch.

Step 3: Title the graph and label the [   ].

Example 3   PROBLEM SOLVING APPLICATION

**Make a double-bar graph to compare
the data in the table.**

1. Understand the Problem
   You are asked to use a graph to
   compare the data given in the table.
   You will need to use all of the
   information given.

Club Memberships			
Club	Art	Music	Science
Boys	12	6	16
Girls	8	14	4

2. Make a Plan

   You can make a [   ] graph to display the two sets of data.

Copyright © by Holt McDougal.
All rights reserved.

130   **Holt McDougal Mathematics**

3. Solve

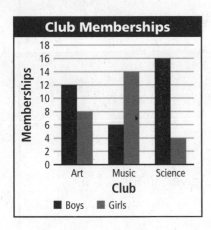

Determine appropriate [____] for both sets of data.

Use the [____] to determine the lengths of the bars. Draw bars of equal [____]. Bars should be in [____]. Use a different [____] for boy memberships and girl memberships. Title the graph and label both [____]. Include a [____] to show what each bar represents.

4. Look Back

You could make two separate graphs, one of boy memberships and one of girl memberships. However, it is easier to compare the two data sets when they are on the same graph.

Check It Out!

1. Use the bar graph to answer the question.

Which biomes in the graph have an average summer temperature of 25°C or greater?

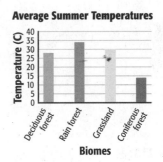

2. Use the data to make a bar graph.

Tickets Sold		
Grade 6	Grade 7	Grade 8
310	215	285

Copyright © by Holt McDougal.
All rights reserved.

Holt McDougal Mathematics

3. Problem Solving Application

Make a double-bar graph to compare the data in the table.

Club Memberships			
Club	Band	Chess	Year Book
Boys	9	14	16
Girls	11	7	15

1. **Understand the Problem**
   You are asked to use a graph to compare the data given in the table.
   You will need to use all of the information given.

2. **Make a Plan**

   You can make a _____ graph to display the two sets
   of data.

3. **Solve**

4. **Look Back**
   You could make two separate graphs, one of boy memberships and one
   of girl memberships. However, it is easier to compare the two data sets
   when they are on the same graph.

Copyright © by Holt McDougal.
All rights reserved.

Holt McDougal Mathematics

Line Plots, Frequency Tables, and Histograms

Lesson Objectives

Organize data in line plots, frequency tables, and histograms

Vocabulary

frequency (p. 304) _____

frequency table (p. 304) _____

_____

line plot (p. 304) _____

_____

histogram (p. 305) _____

_____

Additional Examples

Example 1

Students in Mr. Ray's class recorded their fingerprint patterns. Which type of pattern is most common in Mr. Ray's class?

| whorl | loop | whorl | loop | loop | arch | whorl | arch |
| arch | arch | loop | whorl | arch | whorl | arch | loop |

Make a table to organize the data.

Step 1: Make a ⬚ for each fingerprint pattern.

Step 2: For each fingerprint, make a ⬚ mark in the appropriate column.

Number of Fingerprint Patterns		
Whorl	**Arch**	**Loop**

Most students in Mr. Ray's class have an ⬚ fingerprint.

Copyright © by Holt McDougal.
All rights reserved.

Holt McDougal Mathematics

Example 2

Students collected tennis balls for a project. The number of balls collected by the students is recorded in the table. Make a line plot of the data.

Balls Collected					
10	14	11	16	11	10
14	10	15	15	10	11

Step 1: Draw a ⬚.

Step 2: For each student, use an ⬚ on the number line to represent the number of ⬚ collected.

Example 3

Use the data in the table to make a frequency table with intervals.

Pages Read Last Weekend				
12	15	40	19	7
5	22	34	37	18

Step 1: Choose ⬚ intervals.

Step 2: Find the number of data values in each ⬚. Write these numbers in the "Frequency" row.

Pages Read Last Weekend				
Number				
Frequency				

Example 4

Use the frequency table from Additional Example 3 to make a histogram.

Step 1: Choose an appropriate [   ] and [   ].

Step 2: Draw a bar for the number of students in each interval. The bars should touch but not overlap.

Step 3: Title the graph and label the axes.

Check It Out!

1. Students in Ms. Gracie's class recorded their fingerprint patterns. Which type of pattern do more students in Ms. Gracie's class have?

whorl	loop	whorl	loop	loop	whorl	whorl	arch
arch	whorl	loop	whorl	arch	whorl	arch	loop

2. Students collected paperclips for a project. The number of paperclips collected by the students is recorded in the table. Make a line plot of the data.

Paperclips Collected					
6	9	7	6	5	7
8	9	6	5	8	10

Copyright © by Holt McDougal.
All rights reserved.

Holt McDougal Mathematics

Ordered Pairs

Lesson Objectives

Graph ordered pairs on a coordinate grid

Vocabulary

coordinate grid (p. 311) _____

_____

ordered pair (p. 311) _____

_____

Additional Examples

Example 1

Name the ordered pair for the location.

A. Gym

Start at (☐ , ☐). Move right ☐ units and then up ☐ units.

The gym is located at (▨ , ▨).

B. Theater

Start at (☐ , ☐). Move right ☐ units and then up ☐ unit.

The theater is located at (▨ , ▨).

C. Park

Start at (☐ , ☐). Move right ☐ units and then up ☐ units.

The park is located at (▨ , ▨).

Copyright © by Holt McDougal.
All rights reserved.

Holt McDougal Mathematics

Example 2

Graph and label each point on a coordinate grid.

A. L (3, 5)

Start at (☐ , ☐).

Move right ☐ units.

Move up ☐ units.

B. M (4, 0)

Start at (☐ , ☐).

Move right ☐ units.

Move up ☐ units.

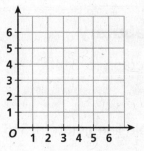

Check It Out!

1. Name the ordered pair for each location.

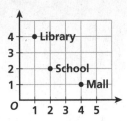

library: ☐

school: ☐

mall: ☐

2. Graph and label each point on a coordinate grid.

T (2, 6) and V (5, 0)

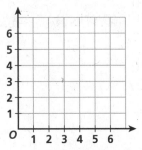

Copyright © by Holt McDougal.
All rights reserved.

Holt McDougal Mathematics

Line Graphs

LESSON
6-7

Lesson Objectives

Display and analyze data in line graphs

Vocabulary

line graph (p. 314) _____

_____

double-line graph (p. 315) _____

_____

Additional Examples

Example 1

Use the data in the table to make a line graph.

Population of New Hampshire	
Year	Population
1650	1,300
1670	1,800
1690	4,200
1700	5,000

Step 1: Place *years* on the horizontal axis and *population* on the vertical axis. Label the axes.

Step 2: Determine an appropriate [＿＿＿] and [＿＿＿] for each axis.

Step 3: Mark a point for each data [＿＿＿]. Connect the points with [＿＿＿] lines.

Step 4: [＿＿＿] the graph.

Copyright © by Holt McDougal.
All rights reserved.

Holt McDougal Mathematics

Example 2

Use the line graph to answer each question.

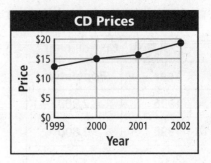

A. In which year did CDs cost the most?

B. About how much did CDs cost in 2000?

$

C. Did CD prices increase or decrease from 1999 to 2002?

Example 3

Use the data in the table to make a double-line graph.

Stock Prices				
	1990	1995	2000	2005
Corporation A	$16	$20	$34	$33
Corporation B	$38	$35	$31	$21

Step 1: Determine an appropriate _____ and _____ .

Step 2: Mark a _____ for each Corporation A value and _____ the points.

Step 3: Mark a _____ for each Corporation B value and _____ the points.

Step 4: Title the graph and label both _____ . Include a _____ .

Copyright © by Holt McDougal.
All rights reserved.

Holt McDougal Mathematics

Check It Out!

1. Use the data in the table to make a line graph.

School District Enrollment	
Year	Population
1996	2,300
1998	2,800
2000	5,200
2002	6,000

2. Use the line graph to answer each question.

In which year did CDs cost the least?

About how much did CDs cost in 1999?

$

Did CD prices increase or decrease
from 2001 to 2002?

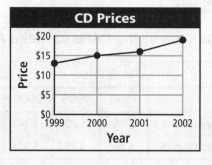

They _____ .

3. Use the data in the table to make a double-line graph.

Stock Prices				
	1990	1995	2000	2005
Corporation C	$8	$16	$20	$28
Corporation D	$35	$22	$14	$7

Copyright © by Holt McDougal.
All rights reserved.

Holt McDougal Mathematics

LESSON 6-8 — Misleading Graphs

Lesson Objectives

Recognize misleading graphs

Additional Examples

Example 1

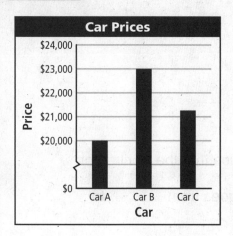

A. Why is this bar graph misleading?

Because the lower part of the ⬜⬜⬜⬜⬜ is missing,

the differences in prices are ⬜⬜⬜⬜.

B. What might people believe from the misleading graph?

People might believe that Cars ⬜ and ⬜ cost $1\frac{1}{2} - 2\frac{1}{2}$ times as much

as Car ⬜. In reality, Cars ⬜ and ⬜ are only a few thousand dollars

more than Car ⬜.

Copyright © by Holt McDougal.
All rights reserved.

Holt McDougal Mathematics

Example 2

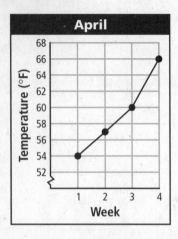

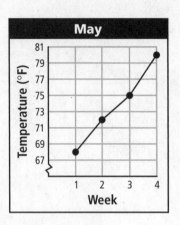

A. Why are these graphs misleading?

If you look at the scale for each graph, you will notice that the April graph

goes from [   ]° to [   ]° and the May graph goes from [   ]° to

[   ]°.

B. What might people believe from these misleading graphs?

People might believe that the [   ] in May were

about the same as the temperatures in [   ]. In reality, the

temperatures in April were about [   ] degrees [   ].

C. Explain why this graph is misleading.

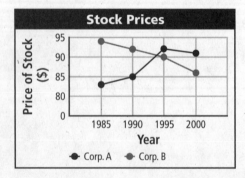

The scale goes from $ [   ] to $ [   ], and then increases by $ [   ].

Copyright © by Holt McDougal.
All rights reserved.

Holt McDougal Mathematics

Check It Out!

1. Why is this bar graph misleading?

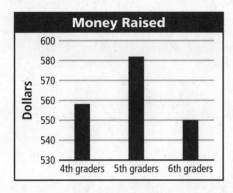

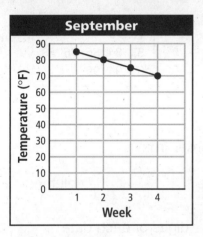

2. Why are these line graphs misleading?

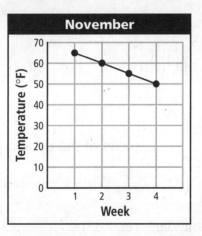

Copyright © by Holt McDougal.
All rights reserved.

Holt McDougal Mathematics

Stem-and-Leaf Plots

Lesson Objectives

Make and analyze stem-and-leaf plots

Vocabulary

stem-and-leaf plot (p. 322) _____

_____

Additional Examples

Example 1

Use the data to make a stem-and-leaf plot.

75   86   83   91   94   88   84   99   79   86

Step 1: Group the data by [____] digits.

| 75 79 |
| 83 84 86 86 88 |
| 91 94 99 |

Step 2: Order the data from [_____] to

[_____].

Step 3: List the [_____] digits of the data in order from [_____]

to [_____]. Write these in the "[_____]" column.

Step 4: For each tens digit, record the [_____] digits of each data

value in order from [_____] to

[_____]. Write these in the

"[_____]" column.

Step 5: Title the graph and add a [_____].

Copyright © by Holt McDougal.
All rights reserved.

Holt McDougal Mathematics

Example 2

Find the least value, greatest value, mean, median, mode, and range of the data.

Stems	Leaves
4	0 0 1 5 7
5	1 1 2 4
6	3 3 3 5 9 9
7	0 4 4
8	3 6 7
9	1 4

Key: 4|0 means 40

The ☐ stem and ☐ leaf give the ☐ value, ☐.

The ☐ stem and ☐ leaf give the ☐ value, ☐.

Use the data values to find the mean $(40 + \ldots + 94) \div 23 =$ ☐.

The ☐ is the middle value in the table, ☐.

To find the ☐, look for the number that occurs most often in a row of leaves. Then identify its stem. The mode is ☐.

The ☐ is the difference between the greatest and the least value. ☐ − ☐ = ☐

Check It Out!

1. Use the data in the table to make a stem-and-leaf plot.

Test Scores				
72	88	64	79	61
84	83	76	74	67

2. Find the least value, greatest value, mean, median, mode, and range of the data.

Stems	Leaves
3	0 2 5 6 8
4	1 1 3 4
5	4 5 6 9 9 9
6	1 2 4
7	5 6 9
8	1 5

Key: 3|0 means 30

Copyright © by Holt McDougal.
All rights reserved.

Holt McDougal Mathematics

Choosing an Appropriate Display

Lesson Objectives

Choose an appropriate way to display data

Example 1

A. The table shows the miles jogged by five boxers. Which graph would be more appropriate to show the data—a line plot or a line graph? Draw the more appropriate graph.

Boxer	Al	Bo	Max	Jo	Ty
Miles	12	17	10	18	17

Think: Is the information in the table describing a change over _____?

Can the information in the table be placed on a _____?

The table shows the number of _____ the boxers jogged. The data

should be displayed on a _____ with _____ showing the

frequencies of values. So a _____ is more appropriate than

a _____.

Copyright © by Holt McDougal.
All rights reserved.

Holt McDougal Mathematics

B. The table shows the heights of some plants. Which graph would be more appropriate to show the data—a bar graph or a stem-and-leaf plot? Draw the more appropriate graph.

Height of Plants (ft)					
11	27	14	35	11	26

Think: Can the information in the table be placed separated by

[   ]? The table shows the [   ] of plants. The data

should be displayed on a [   ]. So a

[   ] is more appropriate than a [   ].

Check It Out!

1. The table shows the temperatures for a city over a 5-day period. Which graph would be more appropriate to show the data—a bar graph or a line graph? Draw the more appropriate graph.

Day	Mon	Tues	Wed	Thurs	Fri
Temperature (°F)	65	72	70	68	75

Copyright © by Holt McDougal.
All rights reserved.

Holt McDougal Mathematics

CHAPTER 6

Chapter Review

6-1 Making a Table

1. On Thursday, 198 people attended the play. On Friday night, 234 people attended the play. On Saturday, 278 people attended the play. On Sunday, 156 people attended the play. Use this data to make a table.

2. Use your table from Exercise 1 to describe attendance change over time.

6-2 Mean, Median, Mode, and Range

Find the mean, median, mode, and range of each data set.

3.

Bowling Scores		
89	133	123

4.

Number of Seconds in Each Commercial				
29	18	45	60	18

5.

Distance (km)							
8	11	8	4	12	6	9	6

6.

Homework Scores							
21	18	24	16	12	23	20	18

7. Margie's first six test scores were 88, 98, 82, 86, 88, and 98. Create a table using this data. Then find the mean, median, mode, and range.

Copyright © by Holt McDougal.
All rights reserved.

Holt McDougal Mathematics

6-3 Additional Data and Outliers

The table shows the number of miles of Interstate 70 in the states of the Great Plains and Midwest.

CO	IL	IN	KA	MD	MO	OH	PA	UT	WV
451	126	157	424	94	252	226	168	232	14

8. What is the median number of miles of Interstate 70 in the states through which the interstate passes?

9. What is the mean number of miles, to the nearest mile, of Interstate 70 in the states through which the interstate passes?

10. What is the mean number of miles, to the nearest mile, of Interstate 70 in the states excluding West Virginia?

6-4 Bar Graphs

Use the bar graph to answer each question.

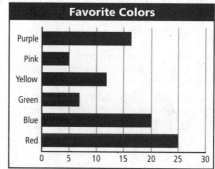

11. Which two colors were the favorites of the most children?

12. Which color received 5 times fewer votes than red?

13. Write a sentence to compare the number of votes for yellow to the number of votes for blue.

6-5 Line Plots, Frequency Tables, and Histograms

Use the line plot to answer each question.

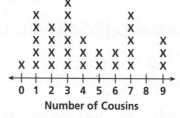

14. How many people were surveyed in all?

15. What are the mode and range of the data?

16. How many people surveyed have less than 4 cousins?

Copyright © by Holt McDougal.
All rights reserved.

Holt McDougal Mathematics

6-6 Ordered Pairs

Graph and label each point on a coordinate grid.

17. $K(2, 6)$ **18.** $W(1, 3)$ **19.** $L(9, 0)$ **20.** $D(5, 7)$

21. The coordinates (7, 5), (2, 5), and (2, 0) form three of the corners of a square. What are the coordinates of the fourth corner?

6-7 Line Graphs

22. Use the data in the table to make a line graph.

Average High Temperature in Rome, Indiana (°F)											
Jan.	Feb.	Mar.	Apr.	May	Jun.	Jul.	Aug	Sep.	Oct.	Nov.	Dec.
42	46	55	59	68	72	82	89	77	65	48	48

Use the line graph you made in Exercise 22 to answer each question.

23. Did the average temperature in Rome, Indiana increase or decrease from July to August?

24. Which month has the lowest average temperature in Rome, Indiana?

6-8 Misleading Graphs

25. Olivia made a line graph of temperatures from Exercise 22 using a vertical scale of 0, 40, 50, 55, 60, 65, 70, 80, 90. Explain why her line graph was misleading.

26. Why is the bar graph misleading? What might people believe from this misleading graph?

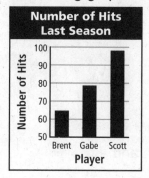

6-9 Stem-and-Leaf Plots

27. Use the data in the temperature table in Exercise 22 to make a stem-and-leaf plot.

28. Use the stem-and-leaf plot you made in Exercise 27 to find the median, mode, and range average temperature in Rome, Indiana.

6-10 Choosing an Appropriate Display

29. Would it be also be appropriate to present the data about cousins in Exercises 14 – 16 in a bar graph? Explain.

Copyright © by Holt McDougal.
All rights reserved.
Holt McDougal Mathematics

Big Ideas

Answer these question to summarize the important concepts from Chapter 6 in your own words.

1. Explain how to find the median of a data set with an even number of data values.

2. Explain how to make a bar graph from a given data set.

3. Explain the similarities and differences between a bar graph and a histogram.

4. Explain how to graph the point $(6, 3\frac{1}{2})$.

5. Explain when you should use a line plot, line graph, bar graph, histogram, or a stem-and-leaf plot to display data.

For more review of Chapter 6:

- Complete the Chapter 6 Study Guide and Review on pages 332–334 of your textbook.

- Complete the Ready to Go On quizzes on pages 296 and 328 of your textbook.

Copyright © by Holt McDougal.
All rights reserved.

Holt McDougal Mathematics

Ratios and Rates

Lesson Objectives

Write ratios and rates and find unit rates

Vocabulary

ratio (p. 342) _____

_____

equivalent ratios (p. 342) _____

_____

rate (p. 343) _____

_____

unit rate (p. 343) _____

_____

Additional Examples

Example 1

Use the table to write each ratio.

Animals at the Vet	
Cats	5
Dogs	7
Rabbits	2

A. cats to rabbits

	or		or				to	

B. dogs to total number of pets

	or		or				to	

C. total number of pets to cats

	or		or				to	

Copyright © by Holt McDougal.
All rights reserved.

Holt McDougal Mathematics

Example 2

Write three equivalent ratios to compare the number of diamonds to the number of spades in the pattern.

$\dfrac{\text{number of diamonds}}{\text{number of spades}} = \dfrac{\boxed{}}{\boxed{}}$ There are $\boxed{}$ diamonds and $\boxed{}$ spades.

$\dfrac{3}{6} = \dfrac{3 \div 3}{6 \div 3} = \dfrac{\boxed{}}{\boxed{}}$ There is $\boxed{}$ diamond for every $\boxed{}$ spades.

$\dfrac{3}{6} = \dfrac{3 \cdot 3}{6 \cdot 3} = \dfrac{\boxed{}}{\boxed{}}$ If you triple the pattern, there will be $\boxed{}$ diamonds for $\boxed{}$ spades.

So, $\boxed{}$, $\boxed{}$, and $\boxed{}$ are equivalent ratios.

Example 3

A 3-pack of paper towels costs $2.79. A 6-pack costs $5.46. Which is the better deal?

$\dfrac{\$2.79}{3 \text{ rolls}}$ Write the $\boxed{}$.

$\dfrac{\$2.79 \div 3}{3 \text{ rolls} \div 3}$ Divide both terms by $\boxed{}$.

$\dfrac{\boxed{}}{1 \text{ roll}}$ $\$\boxed{}$ for 1 roll.

$\dfrac{\$5.46}{6 \text{ rolls}}$ Write the $\boxed{}$.

$\dfrac{\$5.46 \div 6}{6 \text{ rolls} \div 6}$ Divide both terms by $\boxed{}$.

$\dfrac{\boxed{}}{1 \text{ roll}}$ $\$\boxed{}$ for 1 roll.

The $\boxed{}$-pack is the better deal.

Copyright © by Holt McDougal.
All rights reserved.

Holt McDougal Mathematics

Check It Out!

1. Use the table to write the ratio.

birds to total number of pets

Animals at the Vet	
Birds	6
Hamsters	9
Snakes	3

2. Write three equivalent ratios to compare the number of triangles to the number of hearts in the pattern.

3. A 3-pack of juice boxes costs $2.10. A 9-pack costs $5.58. Which is the better deal?

Copyright © by Holt McDougal.
All rights reserved.

Holt McDougal Mathematics

Using Tables to Explore Equivalent Ratios and Rates

Lesson Objectives

Use a table to find equivalent ratios and rates

Additional Examples

Example 1

Use a table to find three equivalent ratios.

A. $\frac{6}{7}$

original   6 · 2   6 · 3   6 · 4

ratio

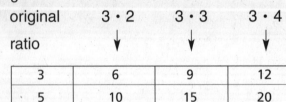

6	12	18	24
7	14	21	28

7 · 2   7 · 3   7 · 4

Multiply the numerator and the denominator by ☐, ☐, and ☐.

The ratios $\frac{6}{7}$, ☐, ☐, and ☐ are equivalent.

B. $\frac{3}{5}$

original   3 · 2   3 · 3   3 · 4

ratio

3	6	9	12
5	10	15	20

5 · 2   5 · 3   5 · 4

Multiply the numerator and the denominator by ☐, ☐, and ☐.

The ratios $\frac{3}{5}$, ☐, ☐, and ☐ are equivalent.

Copyright © by Holt McDougal.
All rights reserved.

Holt McDougal Mathematics

Example 2

Several groups of friends are going to take a shuttle bus to the park. The table shows how much the different groups will pay in all. Predict how much a group of 15 friends will pay.

Number in Group	6	12	18
Bus Fare ($)	12	24	36

12 < ⬚ < 18; therefore, the group will pay between ⬚ and ⬚.

The ratio $\frac{6}{12}$ is equivalent to ⬚, and ⬚ is a factor of 15.

⬚ · 3 = 15   Multiply the numerator and denominator by the same factor, ⬚.

⬚ · $6 = ⬚

A group of 15 friends would pay ⬚.

Check It Out!

1. Use a table to find three equivalent ratios.

   $\frac{2}{9}$

2. Several groups of friends are going to take a shuttle bus to the park. The table shows how much the different groups will pay in all. Predict how much a group of 8 friends will pay.

Number in Group	2	6	10
Amount Paid ($)	8	24	40

Copyright © by Holt McDougal.
All rights reserved.

Holt McDougal Mathematics

Proportions

Lesson Objectives

Write and solve proportions

Vocabulary

proportion (p. 352) _____

_____

Additional Examples

Example 1

Write a proportion for the model.

First write the ratio of ⬚⬚⬚⬚⬚⬚ to ⬚⬚⬚⬚⬚⬚ .

$$\frac{\text{number of hearts}}{\text{number of stars}} = \frac{\boxed{}}{\boxed{}}$$

Next separate the hearts and stars into two ⬚⬚⬚⬚⬚ groups.

Now write the ratio of ⬚⬚⬚⬚⬚⬚ to ⬚⬚⬚⬚⬚⬚ in each group.

$$\frac{\text{number of hearts}}{\text{number of stars}} = \frac{\boxed{}}{\boxed{}}$$

A proportion shown by the model is ⬚⬚⬚⬚⬚⬚ .

Copyright © by Holt McDougal.
All rights reserved.

Holt McDougal Mathematics

Example 2

Find the missing value in the proportion $\frac{5}{6} = \frac{n}{18}$.

$$\frac{5}{6} \diagup\!\!\!\!\diagdown \frac{n}{18}$$

Find the cross [＿＿＿＿＿].

$6 \cdot n = 5 \cdot 18$ The cross products are [＿＿＿＿].

[＿＿＿] = [＿＿＿] n is multiplied by 6.

$\frac{6n}{6} = \frac{90}{6}$ [＿＿＿＿＿] both sides by [＿＿] to

undo the [＿＿＿＿＿].

$n =$ [＿＿＿]

Example 3

According to the label, 1 tablespoon of plant fertilizer should be used per 6 gallons of water. How many tablespoons of fertilizer would you use for 4 gallons of water?

$\dfrac{1 \text{ tbsp}}{6 \text{ gal}} = \dfrac{f}{4 \text{ gal}}$ Let [＿＿] be the amount of fertilizer for [＿＿] gallons of water.

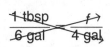

Write a [＿＿＿＿＿].

$6 \cdot f = 1 \cdot 4$ The cross products are [＿＿＿＿].

[＿＿＿] = [＿＿] f is multiplied by 6.

$\dfrac{6f}{6} = \dfrac{4}{6}$ [＿＿＿＿＿] both sides by [＿＿] to undo the [＿＿＿＿＿].

$f =$ Write your answer in simplest form.

You would use [＿＿] tbsp of fertilizer for 4 gallons of water.

Copyright © by Holt McDougal.
All rights reserved.

Holt McDougal Mathematics

Check It Out!

1. Write a proportion for the model.

2. Find the missing value in the proportion.

$$\frac{3}{5} = \frac{n}{15}$$

3. To make a certain shade of pink paint, mix 8 gallons of white paint with 3 gallons of red paint. How many gallons of white paint would you use for 15 gallons of red paint?

Copyright © by Holt McDougal.
All rights reserved.

Holt McDougal Mathematics

Similar Figures

Lesson Objectives

Use proportions to find missing measures in similar figures

Vocabulary

corresponding sides (p. 356) _____

_____

corresponding angles (p. 356) _____

_____

similar (p. 356) _____

Additional Examples

Example 1

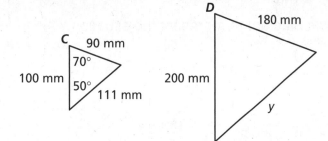

The two triangles are similar. Find the missing length _y_ and the measure of ∠_D_.

$$\frac{100}{200} = \frac{111}{y}$$ Write a [_____] using

[_____] side lengths.

$200 \cdot 111 = 100 \cdot y$ The cross products are [_____].

[_____] $= 100y$ _y_ is multiplied by 100.

$$\frac{22{,}200}{100} = \frac{100y}{100}$$ [_____] both sides by [____] to

undo the [_____].

[_____] mm = _y_

Angle _D_ is congruent to angle [____], and m∠[____] = 70°.

m∠_D_ = [_____]

Example 2 **PROBLEM SOLVING APPLICATION**

This reduction is similar to a picture that Katie painted. The height of the actual painting is 54 centimeters. What is the width of the actual painting?

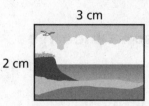

3 cm

2 cm

1. **Understand the Problem**

   The answer will be the [＿＿＿] of the actual painting.
   List the important information:

   • The actual painting and the reduction above are [＿＿＿＿＿].

   • The reduced painting is [＿] cm tall and [＿] cm wide.

   • The actual painting is [＿] cm tall.

2. **Make a Plan**

   Draw a diagram to represent the situation.

   Reduced

   2 [＿＿] 3

   Actual

   54 [＿＿] w

   Use the corresponding sides to write a [＿＿＿＿＿].

3. **Solve**

   $\dfrac{2 \text{ cm}}{54 \text{ cm}} = \dfrac{3 \text{ cm}}{w \text{ cm}}$ Write a [＿＿＿＿＿].

   $54 \cdot 3 = 2 \cdot w$ The cross products are [＿＿＿＿].

   [＿＿] = [＿＿]   *w* is multiplied by 2.

   $\dfrac{162}{2} = \dfrac{2w}{2}$ [＿＿＿＿＿] both sides by [＿] to undo the [＿＿＿＿＿].

   [＿＿＿] = *w*

   The width of the actual painting is [＿＿] cm.

4. **Look Back**

   Estimate to check your answer. The ratio of the heights is about 2:50 or 1:25. The ratio of the widths is about 3:90, or 1:30. Since these ratios are close to each other, 81 cm is a reasonable answer.

Copyright © by Holt McDougal.
All rights reserved.

Holt McDougal Mathematics

Check It Out!

1. The two triangles are similar. Find the missing length *y* and the measure of ∠*B*.

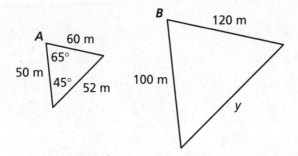

2. This reduction is similar to a picture that Marty painted. The height of the actual painting is 39 inches. What is the width of the actual painting?

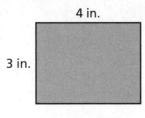

Indirect Measurement

Lesson Objectives

Use proportions and similar figures to find unknown measures

Vocabulary

indirect measurement (p. 360) _____

_____

Additional Examples

Example 1

Use the similar triangles to find the height of the tree.

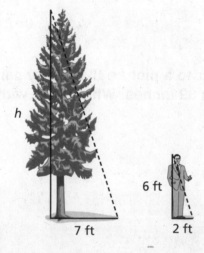

h

6 ft

7 ft   2 ft

$\dfrac{6}{h} = \dfrac{2}{7}$ Write a ⬚ using

⬚ sides.

$h \cdot 2 = 6 \cdot 7$ The cross products are ⬚.

⬚ = ⬚ h is multiplied by 2.

$\dfrac{2h}{2} = \dfrac{42}{2}$ ⬚ both sides by ⬚ to undo the

⬚.

$h =$ ⬚

The tree is ⬚ feet tall.

Copyright © by Holt McDougal.
All rights reserved.

Holt McDougal Mathematics

Example 2

A rocket casts a shadow that is 91.5 feet long. A 4-foot model rocket casts a shadow that is 3 feet long. How tall is the rocket?

$$\frac{h}{4} = \frac{91.5}{3}$$

Write a ⬜ using

⬜ sides.

$$4 \times 91.5 = h \times 3$$

The cross products are ⬜.

⬜ = ⬜ h is multiplied by 3.

$$\frac{366}{3} = \frac{3h}{3}$$

⬜ both sides by ⬜ to undo the

⬜.

⬜ = h

The rocket is ⬜ feet tall.

Check It Out!

1. Use the similar triangles to find the height of the tree.

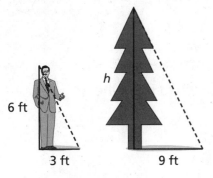

6 ft h

3 ft   9 ft

2. A building casts a shadow that is 72.5 feet long when a 4-foot model building casts a shadow that is 2 feet long. How tall is the building?

Copyright © by Holt McDougal.
All rights reserved.

Holt McDougal Mathematics

Scale Drawings and Maps

Lesson Objectives

Read and use map scales and scale drawings

Vocabulary

scale drawing (p. 364) _____

_____

scale (p. 364) _____

_____

Additional Examples

 Example 1

The scale on a map is 4 in: 1 mi. On the map, the distance between two towns is 20 in. What is the actual distance?

$\dfrac{4 \text{ in.}}{1 \text{mi.}} = \dfrac{20 \text{ in.}}{x \text{ mi}}$
Write a [_____] using the

[_____]. Let x be the actual number of miles

between the two towns.

$1 \cdot 20 = 4 \cdot x$
The cross products are [_____].

[____] = [____]
x is multiplied by 4.

$\dfrac{20}{4} = \dfrac{4x}{4}$
[_____] both sides by [__] to undo the

[_____].

[____] $= x$

The actual distance between the two towns is miles.

Copyright © by Holt McDougal.
All rights reserved.

Holt McDougal Mathematics

Example 2

A. If a drawing of the planets was made using the scale 1 in:30 million km, the distance from Mars to Jupiter on the drawing would be about 18.3 in. What is the actual distance from Mars to Jupiter?

$$\frac{1 \text{ in.}}{30 \text{ million km}} = \frac{18.3 \text{ in.}}{x \text{ million km}}$$

Write a ⬚. Let x be the actual distance from Mars to Jupiter.

$$30 \cdot 18.3 = 1 \cdot x$$

The cross products are ⬚.

$$\boxed{} = x$$

The actual distance from Mars to Jupiter is about ⬚ million km.

B. The actual distance from Earth to Mars is about 78 million kilometers. How far apart should they be drawn?

$$\frac{1 \text{ in.}}{30 \text{ million km}} = \frac{x \text{ in.}}{78 \text{ million km}}$$

Write a ⬚. Let x be the distance from Earth to Mars on the drawing.

$$30 \cdot x = 1 \cdot 78$$

The cross products are ⬚.

$$\boxed{} = \boxed{}$$

x is multiplied by 30.

$$\frac{30x}{30} = \frac{78}{30}$$

⬚ both sides by ⬚ to undo the ⬚.

$$x = \boxed{}$$

Earth and Mars should be drawn ⬚ inches apart.

Check It Out!

1. The scale on a map is 3 in:1 mi. On the map, the distance between two cities is 18 in. What is the actual distance?

Copyright © by Holt McDougal.
All rights reserved.

Holt McDougal Mathematics

Percents

Lesson Objectives

Write percents as decimals and as fractions

Vocabulary

percent (p. 371) _____

_____

Additional Examples

Example 1

Use a 10-by-10 square grid to model 17%.

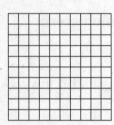

A 10-by-10 square grid has [ ] squares.

17% means "17 out of [ ]" or [ ].

Shade [ ] squares out of [ ] squares.

Example 2

Write 35% as a fraction in simplest form.

$35\% = \dfrac{35}{100}$ Write the percent as a fraction with a denominator of [ ].

$\dfrac{35 \div 5}{100 \div 5} =$ [ ]   Write the fraction in simplest form.

Written as a fraction, 35% is [ ].

Copyright © by Holt McDougal.
All rights reserved.

Holt McDougal Mathematics

Example 3

Janell has 20% body fat. Write 20% as a fraction in simplest form.

$20\% = \dfrac{20}{100}$ Write the percent as a [＿＿＿＿] with a

denominator of [＿＿].

$\dfrac{20 \div 20}{100 \div 20} =$ [＿＿]   Write the fraction in simplest form.

Written as a fraction, 20% is [＿＿].

Example 4

Write 56% as a decimal.

$56\% = \dfrac{56}{100}$ Write the percent as a [＿＿＿＿] with a

denominator of [＿＿].

$$100\overline{)56.00}$$
$$-\underline{50\ 0}$$
$$6\ 00$$
$$-\underline{6\ 00}$$
$$0$$

Write the fraction as a decimal.

Written as a decimal, 56% is [＿＿].

Copyright © by Holt McDougal.
All rights reserved.

Holt McDougal Mathematics

Example 5

Water made up 85% of the fluids that Kirk drank yesterday. Write 85% as a decimal.

85% = [ ]   Write the percent as a [ ] with

a denominator of [ ] .

85 ÷ 100 = [ ]   Write the [ ] as a decimal.

Written as a decimal, 85% is [ ] .

Check It Out!

1. Use a 10-by-10 square grid to model 26%.

2. Write 65% as a fraction in simplest form.

3. Timmy is a football player with 10% body fat. Write 10% as a fraction in simplest form.

4. Write 32% as a decimal.

5. Water made up 95% of the fluids that Lisa drank yesterday. Write 95% as a decimal.

Copyright © by Holt McDougal.
All rights reserved.

Holt McDougal Mathematics

Percents, Decimals, and Fractions

Lesson Objectives

Write decimals and fractions as percents

Additional Examples

Example 1

Write each decimal as a percent.
Method 1: Use place value.

A. 0.7

$$0.7 = \boxed{}$$ Write the decimal as a $\boxed{}$.

$$\frac{7 \times 10}{10 \times 10} = \boxed{}$$ Write an $\boxed{}$ fraction with

$\boxed{}$ as the denominator.

$$\boxed{} = \boxed{}$$ Write the $\boxed{}$ with a percent symbol.

Method 2: Multiply by 100.

B. 0.4118

$$0.4118 \cdot \boxed{}$$ Multiply by $\boxed{}$.

   Add the percent symbol.

Example 2

Write each fraction as a percent.
Method 1: Write an equivalent fraction with a denominator of 100.

A. $\frac{9}{25}$

$$\frac{9 \times 4}{25 \times 4} = \boxed{}$$ Write an $\boxed{}$ fraction with

$\boxed{}$ as the denominator.

$$\boxed{} = \boxed{}$$ Write the $\boxed{}$ with a

percent symbol.

Copyright © by Holt McDougal.
All rights reserved.

Holt McDougal Mathematics

Write each fraction as a percent.

Method 2: Use division to write the fraction as a decimal.

B. $\frac{3}{20}$

[   ]

$20\overline{)3.00}$
$\underline{-2\,0}$
$1\,00$
$\underline{-1\,00}$
0

0.15 = [   ]

Divide the [   ] by the
[   ].

Multiply by [   ] by moving the decimal point

[   ] two places. Add the percent symbol.

Example 3

One year, $\frac{7}{25}$ of people with home offices were self-employed. What percent of people with home offices were self-employed?

$\frac{7}{25}$

$\frac{7 \cdot 4}{25 \cdot 4} = $ [   ]   Find an equivalent fraction with a denominator

of [   ].

$\frac{28}{100} = $ [   ]   Write the [   ] with a percent
sign.

[   ] of people with home offices were self-employed.

Check It Out!

1. Write the decimal as a percent.

   0.023 [   ]

2. Write the fraction as a percent.

   $\frac{7}{50}$ [   ]

3. During the soccer season, $\frac{9}{20}$ of Evan's teammates scored a goal. What percent of Evan's teammates scored a goal?

   [   ]

Copyright © by Holt McDougal.
All rights reserved.

Holt McDougal Mathematics

Percent Problems

Lesson Objectives

Find the missing value in a percent problem

Additional Examples

Example 1

There are 560 students in Ella's school. If 35% of the students participate in after-school sports, how many students participate in after-school sports?

First estimate your answer. Think: 35% = ☐, which is close to $\frac{1}{3}$,

and 560 is close to ☐. So about $\frac{1}{3}$ of the students participate in

after-school sports.

$\frac{1}{3} \cdot 600 = 200$ ⟵ This is the ☐.

Now solve:

$\frac{35}{100} = \frac{s}{560}$ Let *s* represent the number of students who participate in after-school sports.

$100 \cdot s = 35 \cdot 560$ The cross products are ☐.

☐ = ☐   *s* is multiplied by 100.

$\frac{100s}{100} = \frac{19{,}600}{100}$ ☐ both sides of the

equation by ☐ to undo ☐.

$s = $ ☐

Since ☐ is close to your estimate of 200, ☐ is a

reasonable answer.

☐ students participate in after-school sports.

Example 2

Johan is 25% of the way through his exercises. If he has exercised for 20 minutes so far, how much longer does he have to work out?

$$\frac{\%}{100} = \frac{is}{of}$$

He has worked out for 25% of the total time, so

$$\frac{25}{100} = \frac{20}{m}$$

[ ] minutes is [ ] of the total exercise time.

$$100 \cdot 20 = 25 \cdot m$$

The cross products are [ ].

$$[\quad] = [\quad]$$

s is multiplied by 100.

$$\frac{2000}{25} = \frac{25m}{25}$$

[ ] both sides of the equation by

$$[\quad] = m$$

[ ] to undo [ ].

The total exercise time is [ ] minutes. Because [ ] − 20 = [ ],

the remainder of the exercises will take [ ] minutes.

Example 3

Find 36% of 50.

$$36\% = [\quad]$$

Write the percent as a [ ].

$$[\quad] \cdot 50$$

[ ] using the decimal.

$$[\quad]$$

So [ ] is 36% of 50.

Check It Out!

1. There are 480 students in Tisha's school. If 70% of the students are participating in the fundraising program, how many students is that?

[ ]

Copyright © by Holt McDougal.
All rights reserved.

Holt McDougal Mathematics

Applying Percents

Lesson Objectives

Solve percent problems that involve discounts, tips, and sales tax

Vocabulary

discount (p. 384) _____

_____

tip (p. 384) _____

_____

sales tax (p. 384) _____

_____

Additional Examples

Example 1

A clothing store is having a 10% off sale. If Angela wants to buy a sweater whose regular price is $19.95, about how much will she pay for the sweater after the discount?

Step 1: First round $19.95 to $[____].

Step 2: Find 10% of $20 by [_____] [_____] · 20.

(**Hint:** Moving the decimal point one place left is a shortcut.)

10% of 20 = 0.10 · $20 = $[____]

The approximate discount is $[____].[_____] this amount from $20.00 to estimate the cost of the sweater.

$20.00 − $2.00 = $[____]

Angela will pay about $[____] for the sweater.

Copyright © by Holt McDougal.
All rights reserved.

Holt McDougal Mathematics

Example 2

Ben's dinner bill is $7.85. He wants to leave a tip that is 15% of the bill. About how much should his tip be?

Step 1: First round $7.85 to $ ___ .

Step 2: Think: 15% = 10% + 5%

10% of $8 = 0.10 · $8 = $ ___ .

Step 3: 5% = 10% ÷ 2

= $0.80 ÷ 2 = $ ___

Step 4: 15% = ___ % + ___ %

= ___ + ___ = ___

Ben should leave about $ ___ as a tip.

Example 3

Ann is buying a $29.75 dog bed. The sales tax rate is 7%. About how much will the total cost be?

Step 1: First round $29.75 to $ ___ .

Step 2: Think: 7% = 7 · 1%

1% of $30 = 0.01 · $30 = $ ___

Step 3: 7% = 7 · 1%

= 7 · $ ___ = $ ___

The approximate sales tax is $ ___ . ___ this amount to $30 to estimate the total cost of the dog bed.

$30 + $ ___ = $ ___

Ann will pay about $ ___ for the dog bed.

Check It Out!

1. A fishing store is having a 10% off sale. If Gerald wants to buy a fishing pole whose regular price is $39.95, about how much will he pay for the pole after the discount?

2. Fran's breakfast bill is $13.95. She wants to leave a tip that is 20% of the bill. About how much should her tip be?

3. Erik is buying a blanket for $19.83. The sales tax rate is 8%. About how much will the total cost of the blanket be?

Copyright © by Holt McDougal.
All rights reserved.

Holt McDougal Mathematics

Chapter Review

7-1 Ratios and Rates

Use the table to write each ratio.

Jeff's T-Shirt Colors	
Red	4
White	14
Blue	7
Gray	9

1. red shirts to gray shirts

2. blue shirts to white shirts

3. white shirts to total shirts

4. Sunshine Gymnastics charges $60 for a 6-week class. ABC Gymnastics charges $45 for a 4-week class. Which class is the better deal?

7-2 Using Tables to Explore Equivalent Ratios and Rates

Use a table to find three equivalent ratios.

5. $\frac{9}{13}$

6. 25:7

7. 11 to 30

8. Andrew swims laps for exercise. The table shows how long it takes him to swim different numbers of laps. Predict how long it will take him to swim 50 laps.

Number of laps	10	20	30	60	70
Time (min)	5	10	15	30	35

7-3 Proportions

9. Write a proportion for the model.

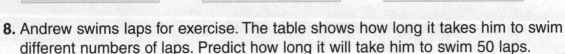

Find the missing value in each proportion.

10. $\frac{p}{42} = \frac{15}{7}$

11. $\frac{5}{9} = \frac{8}{n}$

12. $\frac{2}{a} = \frac{34}{51}$

13. $\frac{3}{10} = \frac{b}{30}$

Copyright © by Holt McDougal.
All rights reserved.

Holt McDougal Mathematics

7-4 Similar Figures

14. The two triangles are similar. Find the missing length *c* and the measure of ∠*Y*.

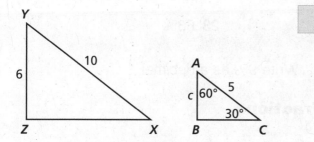

15. Two paintings are similar in size. The larger painting is three times the size of the smaller painting. The smaller painting has a length of 7 feet and a width of 2 feet. What is the length and width of the larger painting?

7-5 Indirect Measurement

16. A 10-foot basketball pole casts a 4-foot shadow. A 4-foot-tall boy is standing by the basketball pole. How long is his shadow?

17. A telephone pole casts a shadow that is 5 m long. A house next to the pole is 18 m tall and casts a 7.5 m shadow. How tall is the telephone pole?

18. A 42-foot-tall building casts a 12-foot shadow. A nearby tree casts an 8-foot shadow. How tall is the tree?

7-6 Scale Drawings and Maps

19. The key on a map is 1 inch = 75 miles. The distance from New York City to Buffalo is 6 inches on the map. How many miles is it from New York City to Buffalo?

20. A model spaceship has a scale of 3 inches = 50 feet. A spaceship is 225 feet long. How long is the model?

Copyright © by Holt McDougal.
All rights reserved.

Holt McDougal Mathematics

7-7 Percents

Write each percent as a fraction in simplest form.

21. 36%

22. 55%

23. 68%

24. The city of Chicago's sales tax is 9%. Write 9% as a decimal.

7-8 Percents, Decimals, and Fractions

Write each decimal as a percent.

25. 0.61

26. 0.0475

27. 0.209

Write each fraction as a percent.

28. $\frac{4}{5}$

29. $\frac{69}{200}$

30. $\frac{9}{15}$

31. A football player completes 11 of 16 passes. What percent of the passes did the football player complete?

7-9 Percent Problems

32. Nick has done 35% of his homework. He has been working for 28 minutes. How long will it take him to complete his homework?

33. Maya's boss wants her to alphabetize 80 files. She has already alphabetized 60 files. What percent of the files has she alphabetized?

34. Find 41% of 120.

35. Find 14% of 60.

36. Find 5% of 650.

7-10 Applying Percents

37. A camping store is having a sale. All tents are 30% off. If the regular price of a tent is $199.00, what is the sale price?

38. Ryan's bill was $52.00. He left a 20% tip. How much was the tip?

39. Melanie bought a dollhouse for $130.00. The sales tax was 6%. What was the total price of the dollhouse including tax?

Copyright © by Holt McDougal.
All rights reserved.

Holt McDougal Mathematics

Big Ideas

Answer these question to summarize the important concepts from Chapter 7 in your own words.

1. Explain how to find an equivalent ratio.

2. Explain how to find the value of n in the proportion $\frac{5}{20} = \frac{n}{35}$.

3. On a map the distance between two cities is 3.5 inches. The scale on the map is 1 inch = 10 miles. Explain how to find the actual distance between the two cities.

4. Explain how to write 45% as a fraction.

5. Explain how to write 0.08 as a percent.

For more review of Chapter 7:

• Complete the Chapter 7 Study Guide and Review on pages 394–396 of your textbook.

• Complete the Ready to Go On quizzes on pages 368 and 390 of your textbook.

Copyright © by Holt McDougal.
All rights reserved.

Holt McDougal Mathematics

Building Blocks of Geometry

Lesson Objectives

Describe figures by using the terms of geometry

Vocabulary

point (p. 406) _____

_____

line (p. 406) _____

_____

plane (p. 406) _____

_____

line segment (p. 407) _____

_____

ray (p. 407) _____

_____

Additional Examples

Example 1

Use the diagram to name each geometric figure.

A. three points

[ ] , [ ] , and [ ]

Five points are labeled: points [ ] , [ ] ,

[ ] , [ ] , and [ ] .

B. two lines

[ ] and [ ]

You can also write $\overrightarrow{RP}$ and $\overrightarrow{RN}$.

Copyright © by Holt McDougal.
All rights reserved.

Holt McDougal Mathematics

Use the diagram to name each geometric figure.

C. a point shared by two lines

point ☐

Point *R* is a point on ☐ and ☐.

D. a plane

plane ☐

Use any ☐ points in the plane that are ☐ on the same line. Write the points in any order.

Example 2

Use the diagram to give a possible name to each figure.

A. three different line segments

☐ , ☐ , and ☐

You can also write ☐ , ☐ , and ☐ .

B. three ways to name the line

☐ , ☐ , and ☐

You can also write ☐ , ☐ , and ☐ .

Check It Out!

1. Use the diagram to name each geometric figure.

two lines

☐ and ☐

2. Use the diagram to give a possible name to each figure.

three different line segments

☐ , ☐ , and ☐ .

Copyright © by Holt McDougal.
All rights reserved.

Holt McDougal Mathematics

Measuring and Classifying Angles

Lesson Objectives

Name, measure, draw, and classify angles

Vocabulary

angle (p. 410) _____

_____

vertex (p. 410) _____

acute angle (p. 411) _____

_____

right angle (p. 411) _____

obtuse angle (p. 411) _____

_____

straight angle (p. 411) _____

Additional Examples

Example 1

**Use a protractor to measure the angle.
Tell what type of angle it is.**

- Place the [   ] point of the

  protractor on the [   ]

  of the angle.

- Place the protractor so that ray [   ] passes through the [   ]° mark.

- Using the scale that starts with [   ]° along ray *GH*, read the measure

  where ray [   ] crosses.

- The measure of ∠*FGH* is [   ]°. Write this as m∠*FGH* = [   ]°.

- Since 120° > 90° and 120° < 180°, the angle is [   ].

Copyright © by Holt McDougal.
All rights reserved.

Holt McDougal Mathematics

Example 2

Use a protractor to draw an angle that measures 80°.

- Draw a [   ] on a sheet of paper.

- Place the [   ] point of the protractor on the endpoint of the [   ].

- Place the [   ] so that the [   ] passes through the [   ]° mark.

- Make a mark at [   ]° above the scale on the [   ].

- Use a straightedge to draw a [   ] from the endpoint of the first ray through the mark you make at [   ]°.

Example 3

Classify each angle as acute, right, obtuse, or straight.

A.

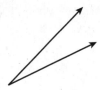

The angle measures [   ] 90°, so it is an [   ] angle.

Copyright © by Holt McDougal.
All rights reserved.

185   Holt McDougal Mathematics

Example 4

A welder used this piece of metal on his project. Classify ∠X, ∠Y, and ∠Z.

∠X [   ]   The angle is marked as a

[   ] angle.

∠Y [   ]   The angle measures more than [   ]°

and less than [   ]°.

∠Z [   ]   The angle measures less than [   ]°.

Check It Out!

1. Use a protractor to measure the angle. Tell what type of angle it is.

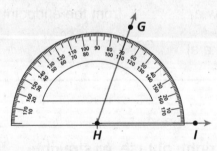

[   ]

2. Classify the angle as acute, right, obtuse, or straight.

[   ]

Copyright © by Holt McDougal.
All rights reserved.

Holt McDougal Mathematics

Angle Relationships

Lesson Objectives

Understand relationships of angles

Vocabulary

congruent angles (p. 416) _____

_____

vertical angles (p. 416) _____

_____

adjacent angles (p. 416) _____

_____

complementary angles (p. 417) _____

_____

supplementary angles (p. 417) _____

_____

Additional Examples

Example 1

Identify the type of each angle pair shown.

A.

∠5 and ∠6 are [   ] each other and

are formed by two [   ] lines.

They are [   ] angles.

B.

∠7 and ∠8 are side by side and have a common

[   ] and [   ].

They are [   ] angles.

Copyright © by Holt McDougal.
All rights reserved.
Holt McDougal Mathematics

Example 2

Find each unknown angle measure.

A. The angles are complementary.

The sum of the measures is ☐°.

$$71° + a = \quad 90°$$
$$\underline{-71°} \qquad \underline{-71°}$$
$$a = \quad \boxed{}°$$

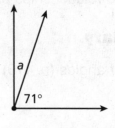

B. The angles are supplementary.

The sum of the measures is ☐°.

$$125° + b = \quad 180°$$
$$\underline{-125°} \qquad \underline{-125°}$$
$$b = \quad \boxed{}°$$

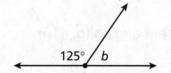

Check It Out!

1. Identify the type of angle pair shown.

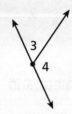

2. Find the unknown angle measure.

Copyright © by Holt McDougal.
All rights reserved.

Holt McDougal Mathematics

Classifying Pairs of Lines

Lesson Objectives

Classify pairs of lines

Vocabulary

parallel lines (p. 420) _____

_____

perpendicular lines (p. 420) _____

_____

skew lines (p. 420) _____

Additional Examples

Example 1

Classify each pair of lines.

A.

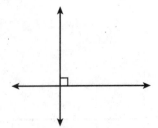

The lines intersect to form [_____]
angles.

They are [_____] .

B.

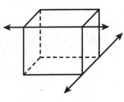

The lines are in different [_____]

and are not [_____] . or

[_____] .

They are [_____] .

Copyright © by Holt McDougal.
All rights reserved.
Holt McDougal Mathematics

C.

The lines are in the same _____

They do not appear to _____.

They are _____.

D.

The lines cross at _____ common point.

They are _____.

Example 2

The handrails on an escalator are in the same plane. What type of line relationship do they represent?

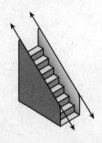

The handrails are in the same _____ and

do not _____.

They are _____.

Check It Out!

1. Classify the pair of lines.

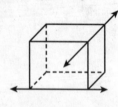

_____

Copyright © by Holt McDougal.
All rights reserved.

Holt McDougal Mathematics

Triangles

Lesson Objectives

Classify triangles and solve problems involving angle and side measures of triangles

Vocabulary

acute triangle (p. 429) _____

_____

_____

obtuse triangle (p. 429) _____

_____

right triangle (p. 429) _____

_____

_____

scalene triangle (p. 430) _____

_____

_____

isosceles triangle (p. 430) _____

_____

_____

equilateral triangle (p. 430) _____

_____

_____

Copyright © by Holt McDougal.
All rights reserved.

Holt McDougal Mathematics

Additional Examples

Example 1

Sara designed this triangular trophy. The measure of ∠E is 38°, and the measure of ∠F is 52°. Classify the triangle.

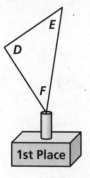

1st Place

To classify the triangle, find the measure

of ∠ [   ] on the trophy.

$m\angle D = 180° - ([]° + []°)$

$m\angle D = 180° - []°$ Subtract the sum of the known angle

$m\angle D = []°$ measures from []°

So the measure of ∠D is []°. Because ΔDEF has one []

angle, the trophy is a [] triangle.

Example 2

Use the diagram to find the measure of the indicated angle.

A. ∠QTR

∠QTR and ∠STR are []

angles, so the sum of m∠QTR and

m∠STR is []°.

$m\angle QTR = 180° - []°$

$= []°$

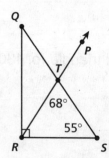

Copyright © by Holt McDougal.
All rights reserved.

Holt McDougal Mathematics

Example 3

Classify the triangle. The sum of the lengths of the sides is 19.5 in.

$c + (6.5 + 6.5) = 19.5$

$c + \boxed{} = 19.5$

$c + 13 - \boxed{} = 19.5 - \boxed{}$

$c = \boxed{}$

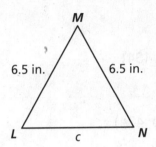

Side c is $\boxed{}$ inches long. Because $\triangle LMN$ has three

$\boxed{}$ sides, it is $\boxed{}$.

Check It Out!

1. Sara designed a triangular trophy. The measures of two of the angles of the triangle are each 22°. Classify the triangle as acute, obtuse, or right.

2. Use the diagram to find the measure of $\angle MON$.

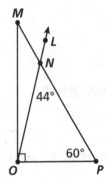

3. Classify the triangle as scalene, isosceles, or equilateral. The sum of the lengths of the sides is 156 in.

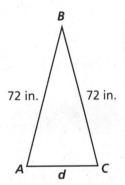

Quadrilaterals

Lesson Objectives

Identify, classify, and compare quadrilaterals

Vocabulary

quadrilateral (p. 434) _____

_____

parallelogram (p. 434) _____

_____

rectangle (p. 434) _____

_____

rhombus (p. 434) _____

_____

square (p. 434) _____

_____

trapezoid (p. 434) _____

_____

Additional Examples

Example 1

Give the most descriptive name for each figure.

A.

The figure is a _____

and a _____.

_____ is the most descriptive name.

Copyright © by Holt McDougal.
All rights reserved.

Holt McDougal Mathematics

B.

The figure is a

_____, a

_____, and a

_____.

_____ is the most descriptive name.

Example 2

Complete the statement.

A. A rectangle can also be called a ___?___.

A rectangle has opposite sides that are _____; it can be

called a _____.

B. A parallelogram cannot be a ___?___.

A parallelogram has opposite sides that are _____; it cannot

be called a _____.

Check It Out!

1. Give the most descriptive name for the figure.

 _____

2. Complete the statement.

A rhombus with four right angles is a ___?___. _____

Copyright © by Holt McDougal.
All rights reserved.

Holt McDougal Mathematics

Polygons

Lesson Objectives

Identify regular and not regular polygons and find the angle measures of regular polygons

Vocabulary

polygon (p. 438) _____

regular polygon (p. 438) _____

diagonal (p. 438) _____

Additional Examples

Example 1

Tell whether each shape is a polygon. If so, give its name and tell whether it appears to be regular or not regular.

A.

The shape is a [ ] plane figure formed by

[ ] or more line segments.

There are [ ] sides and [ ] angles.

All 5 sides do not appear to be congruent.

B.

The shape is a [ ] plane figure formed by

[ ] or more line segments.

There are [ ] sides and [ ] angles.

All sides appear to be congruent.

Copyright © by Holt McDougal.
All rights reserved.

Holt McDougal Mathematics

Example 2 **PROBLEM SOLVING APPLICATION**

Malcolm designed a wall hanging that was a regular 9-sided polygon (called a *nonagon*). What is the measure of each angle of the nonagon?

1. Understand the Problem

The answer will be the measure of each angle in a nonagon.
List the important information:

• A regular nonagon has 9 congruent sides and 9 congruent angles.

2. Make a Plan

Make a table to look for a pattern using regular polygons.

3. Solve

Draw some regular polygons and divide each into triangles.

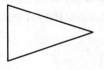

Polygon	Sides	Triangles	Sum of Angle Measures
Triangle	3	☐	☐
Quadrilateral	4	☐	☐ × 180° = ☐
Pentagon	5	☐	☐ × 180° = ☐
Hexagon	6	☐	☐ × 180° = ☐

The number of triangles is always ☐ fewer than the number of sides.

A ☐ can be divided into 9 − ☐ = ☐ triangles.

The sum of the interior angle measures in a nonagon is

☐ × 180° = ☐°.

So the measure of each angle is 1,260° ÷ 9 = ☐°.

4. Look Back

Each angle in a nonagon is obtuse. 140° is a reasonable answer, because an obtuse angle is between 90° and 180°.

Copyright © by Holt McDougal.
All rights reserved.

Holt McDougal Mathematics

Check It Out!

1. Tell whether the shape is a polygon. If so, give its name and tell whether it appears to be regular or not regular.

2. Sara designed a picture that was a regular 6-sided polygon (called a hexagon). What is the measure of each angle of the hexagon?

Copyright © by Holt McDougal.
All rights reserved.

Holt McDougal Mathematics

Geometric Patterns

Lesson Objectives

Recognize, describe, and extend geometric patterns

Additional Examples

Example 1

Identify a possible pattern. Use the pattern to draw the next figure.

A.

Each circle has one more dot than the one to its [____] . The dots are

positioned around the circle from top to bottom and [____] to

[____] .

So the next figure might be [____] .

B.

Each figure has [____] or [____] more circles than the figure to its

[____] .

So the next figure might be [____] .

Copyright © by Holt McDougal.
All rights reserved.

Holt McDougal Mathematics

Example 2

Identify a possible pattern. Use the pattern to draw the missing figure.

A.   , ?

The first figure has ☐ right triangle. The second figure has ☐ right

triangles arranged counterclockwise. The fourth figure has ☐ right

triangles.

So the missing figure might be ☐ .

B.

   ?

The first figure has 1 dot. The second figure is double the first figure

☐. The third figure is double the second figure

☐. The fourth figure could be double the third

figure ☐, and then the fifth figure will be double the

fourth figure ☐.

So the missing figure might be ☐ .

Copyright © by Holt McDougal.
All rights reserved.

Holt McDougal Mathematics

Example 3

Travis is painting a platter. Identify a pattern that Travis is using and draw what the finished platter might look like.

The pattern from inside to outside is [ ] stripe,

[ ] stripe, [ ] stripe, [ ] stripe,

[ ] stripe, [ ] stripe.

Following this pattern, the finished platter might look like this platter.

Check It Out!

1. Identify a possible pattern. Use the pattern to draw the next figure.

   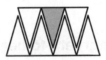

2. Identify a possible pattern. Use the pattern to draw the missing figure.

    ?

Copyright © by Holt McDougal.
All rights reserved.

Holt McDougal Mathematics

Congruent Polygons

Lesson Objectives

Identify congruent figures; use congruence to solve problems

Vocabulary

congruent figures (p. 450) _____

Additional Examples

Example 1

Decide whether the figures in each pair are congruent. If not, explain.

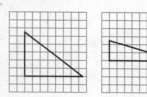

These figures do not have the same

[_____] and they are not the

same [_____].

These figures are [_____].

Example 2

Jodi needs a sleeping pad that is congruent to her sleeping bag. Which sleeping pad should she buy?

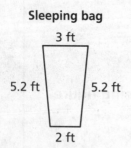

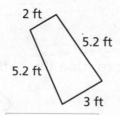

Sleeping bag

3 ft

5.2 ft   5.2 ft

2 ft

Sleeping pad A

2.3 ft

5.2 ft

5.2 ft

1.5 ft

Sleeping pad B

2 ft

5.2 ft

5.2 ft

3 ft

Which pad is the same [_____] and [_____] as the bag?

Both sleeping pads are trapezoids. Pad [____] is the same size as the bag.

Sleeping pad [____] is [_____] to the sleeping bag.

Copyright © by Holt McDougal.
All rights reserved.

Holt McDougal Mathematics

Check It Out!

1. Decide whether the figures in each pair are congruent. If not, explain.

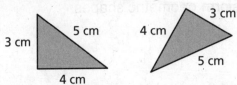

2. Melody needs a frame that is congruent to her flag. Which frame should she buy?

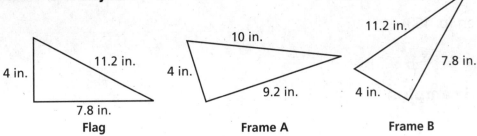

Flag   Frame A   Frame B

Copyright © by Holt McDougal.
All rights reserved.

Holt McDougal Mathematics

Transformations

Lesson Objectives

Use translations, reflections, and rotations to transform geometric shapes

Vocabulary

transformation (p. 453) _____

translation (p. 453) _____

rotation (p. 453) _____

reflection (p. 453) _____

_____

line of reflection (p. 453) _____

_____

Additional Examples

Example 1

Tell whether each is a translation, rotation, or reflection.

A.

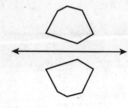

The figure is [_____] over a line.

It is a [_____].

B.

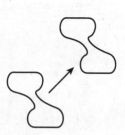

The figure is [_____] along a line.

It is a [_____].

C.

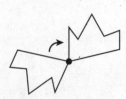

The figure moves [_____] a point.

It is a [_____].

Copyright © by Holt McDougal.
All rights reserved.

Holt McDougal Mathematics

Example 2

Draw each transformation.

A. Draw a 180° rotation about the point shown.

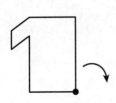

Trace the figure and the point of [   ].

Place your pencil on the point of [   ].

Rotate the figure [   ]°.

Trace the figure in its new location.

B. Draw a horizontal reflection.

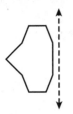

Trace the figure and the line of [   ].

Fold along the on the line of [   ].

Trace the figure in its new location.

Check It Out!

1. Tell whether the transformation is a translation, rotation, or reflection.

2. Draw a horizontal reflection.

Copyright © by Holt McDougal.
All rights reserved.

Holt McDougal Mathematics

Symmetry

Lesson Objectives

Identify symmetry

Vocabulary

line symmetry (p. 457) _____

_____

line of symmetry (p. 457) _____

rotational symmetry (p. 458) _____

_____

Additional Examples

Example 1

Determine whether each dashed line appears to be a line of symmetry.

A.

The two parts of the figure appear to

_____ exactly when _____ or

_____ across the line.

The line _____ to be a line of symmetry.

B.

The two parts of the figure do not appear

_____.

The line _____ to be a line of symmetry.

Example 2

Find all of the lines of symmetry in the regular polygon.

A.

Trace the figure and cut it out.

Fold the figure in [＿＿＿＿] in different ways.

[＿＿＿＿＿＿＿] the lines of symmetry.

[＿＿] lines of symmetry.

B.

Count the lines of symmetry.

[＿＿] lines of symmetry.

Example 3

Find all of the lines of symmetry in the regular polygon.

A. Alaska

B. Arizona

There are [＿＿] lines of symmetry.

[＿＿] line of symmetry

Example 4

Tell whether each figure has rotational symmetry.

A.

Each time the figure is rotated [＿＿] about its center, the image [＿＿＿＿] like the original figure. The figure [＿＿＿＿＿] rotational symmetry.

B.

For any rotation less than [＿＿], the image [＿＿＿＿＿] like the original figure. The figure [＿＿＿＿＿＿] rotational symmetry.

Copyright © by Holt McDougal.
All rights reserved.

Holt McDougal Mathematics

Check It Out!

1. Determine whether the dashed line appears to be a line of symmetry.

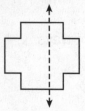

2. Find all the lines of symmetry in the regular polygon.

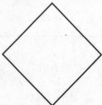

3. Find all of the lines of symmetry in the design.

4. Tell whether the figure has rotational symmetry.

Copyright © by Holt McDougal.
All rights reserved.

Holt McDougal Mathematics

8-1 Building Blocks of Geometry

Use the diagram to find a name for each geometric figure described.

1. three points on the same line

2. two different rays

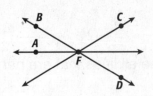

8-2 Measuring and Classifying Angles

Classify each angle as acute, right, obtuse, or straight.

3.

4.

5.

Use a protractor to draw an angle with each given measure.

6. 45°

7. 120°

8. 95°

8-3 Angle Relationships

Use the figure for Exercise 9.

9. If the m∠8 is 54°, what are the measures of ∠5, ∠6, and ∠7?

Find the measure of the angle that is complementary to each given angle.

10. 33°

11. 64°

12. 75°

13. 17°

Copyright © by Holt McDougal.
All rights reserved.

Holt McDougal Mathematics

8-4 Classifying Pairs of Lines

The lines in the figure intersect to form a rectangular box.

14. Name all lines that are parallel to $\overleftrightarrow{DC}$.

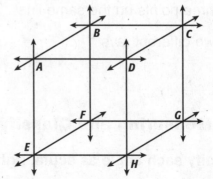

15. Name all lines that are perpendicular to $\overleftrightarrow{AD}$.

16. Name a pair of lines that are skew.

8-5 Triangles

Classify each triangle using the given information.

17. The perimeter of the triangle is 160 cm.

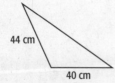

44 cm

40 cm

18. The perimeter of the triangle is 28.6 ft.

8 ft

10.3 ft

The lengths of two sides are given for $\triangle ABC$. Calculate the length of the third side and classify each triangle.

19. $AB = 14$ cm; $BC = 14$ cm;

sum = 42 cm

20. $AB = 4\frac{1}{8}$ in.; $BC = 5\frac{5}{8}$ in.;

sum = $16\frac{7}{8}$

8-6 Quadrilaterals

Complete each statement.

24. A rectangle with 4 congruent sides is a _____?_____.

25. A quadrilateral with exactly two parallel sides is a _____?_____.

Copyright © by Holt McDougal.
All rights reserved.

Holt McDougal Mathematics

Determine if the given statements are sometimes, always or never true.

26. A square is a parallelogram.

27. A parallelogram is a rectangle.

8-7 Polygons

Explain why each shape is NOT a polygon.

28.

29.

30.

Classify each of the following polygons as either *always* regular, *sometimes* regular, or *never* regular.

		Always	Sometimes	Never
31.	Rhombus	?	?	?
32.	Rectangle	?	?	?
33.	Right Triangle	?	?	?
34.	Parallelogram	?	?	?

8-8 Geometric Patterns

Draw the next figure in the pattern.

35.

36.

37.

Copyright © by Holt McDougal.
All rights reserved.

Holt McDougal Mathematics

8-9 Congruent Polygons

Decide whether the figures in each pair are congruent. If not, explain.

38.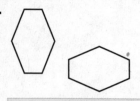

39.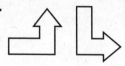

40.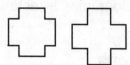

8-10 Transformations

Tell whether each is a translation, rotation, or reflection.

41.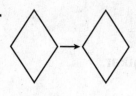

42.

43.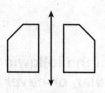

8-11 Symmetry

Find all the lines of symmetry in each regular polygon.

44.

45.

46.

Determine whether each dashed line appears to be a line of symmetry.

47.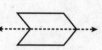

48.

49.

Copyright © by Holt McDougal.
All rights reserved.

Holt McDougal Mathematics

Big Ideas

Answer these questions to summarize the important concepts from Chapter 8 in your own words.

1. Explain how to measure an angle with a protractor.

2. Explain why the angle measures 55° and 35° are complementary angles.

3. Two angle measures in a triangle are 85° and 62°. Explain how to find the measure of the third angle in the triangle.

4. Explain how to draw a 90° clockwise rotation about a point.

5. Explain how to find all the lines of symmetry in a regular octagon.

For more review of Chapter 8:

- Complete the Chapter 8 Study Guide and Review on pages 468–470 of your textbook.

- Complete the Ready to Go On quizzes on pages 426, 448, and 464 of your textbook.

Copyright © by Holt McDougal.
All rights reserved.

Holt McDougal Mathematics

Understanding Customary Units of Measure

Lesson Objectives

Understand and select appropriate customary units of measure

Vocabulary

customary system (p. 480) _____

Additional Examples

Example 1

What unit of measure provides the best estimate?

A. A doorway is about 7 _____ high.

Think: The height of a doorway is about 7 times the distance from your

[_____] to your [_____]. A doorway is about 7 [_____] high.

B. A calculator is about 6 _____ long. Think: The length of a calculator is

about 6 times the width of your [_____]. A calculator is about

6 [_____] long.

Example 2

What unit of measure provides the best estimate?

A. A loaf of bread weighs about 16 _____.

Think: A loaf of bread has the weight of 16 [_____] of bread.

A loaf of bread weighs about 16 [_____].

B. A bike could weigh 20 _____.

Think: A bike could have the weight of 20 [_____] of bread.

A bike could weigh 20 [_____].

Copyright © by Holt McDougal.
All rights reserved.

Holt McDougal Mathematics

Example 3

What unit of measure provides the best estimate?

A large watercooler holds about 10 _____ of water.

Think: A large watercooler holds about 10 [_____] containers of milk.

A large watercooler holds about 10 [_____].

Example 4

Use a ruler to measure the length of the line segment to the nearest half, fourth, or eighth of an inch.

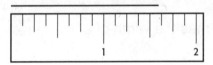

The line segment is between [____] and [____] in. It is closer to [____] in.

The length of the line segment is about [____] in.

Check It Out!

1. A student's desk is about 3 _____ wide.

2. A DVD remote control weighs about 8 _____.

3. A small fish aquarium holds about 20 _____ of water.

Copyright © by Holt McDougal.
All rights reserved.

Holt McDougal Mathematics

Understanding Metric Units of Measure

Lesson Objectives

Understand and select appropriate metric units of measure

Vocabulary

metric system (p. 484) _____

_____

Additional Examples

Example 1

What unit of measure provides the best estimate?

A. A ballpoint pen is about 14 _____ long.

Think: The length of a ballpoint pen is about 14 times the width of a

[_____].

A ballpoint pen is about 14 [_____] long.

B. A football field is about 100 _____ long.

Think: The length of a football field is about 100 times the width of a

[_____].

A football field is about 100 [_____] long.

Example 2

What unit of measure provides the best estimate?

An orange has a mass of about 600 _____.

Think: An orange has the mass of about 600 large [_____].

An orange has a mass of about 600 [_____].

Copyright © by Holt McDougal.
All rights reserved.

Holt McDougal Mathematics

Example 3

What unit of measure provides the best estimate?

An ice cream scoop holds about 100 _____.

Think: An ice cream scoop holds about 100 ⬜ of water.

An ice cream scoop holds about 100 ▨ .

Example 4

Use a ruler to measure the length of the line segment to the nearest centimeter.

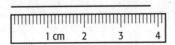

The line segment is between ⬜ cm and ⬜ cm. It is closer to ⬜ cm.

The length of the line segment is about ▨ cm.

Check It Out!

1. What unit of measure provides the best estimate?

A doorway is about 3 _____ high.

▨

2. What unit of measure provides the best estimate?

An encyclopedia has a mass of about 4 _____.

▨

3. What unit of measure provides the best estimate?

There are about 2 _____ of lemonade in a full pitcher.

▨

Copyright © by Holt McDougal.
All rights reserved.

Holt McDougal Mathematics

Converting Customary Units

Lesson Objectives

Convert customary units of measure

Additional Examples

Example 1

A. Convert 9 yards to feet.

$9 \text{ yd} \times \dfrac{\boxed{} \text{ ft}}{1 \text{ yd}}$

$9 \text{ yd} = \boxed{} \text{ ft}$

Think: feet to yards — $\boxed{}$ ft = 1 yd,

so use $\dfrac{\boxed{} \text{ ft}}{1 \text{ yd}}$.

Multiply 9 yd by the conversion factor.

Cancel the common unit, $\boxed{}$.

B. Convert 10,000 pounds to tons.

$10{,}000 \text{ lb} \times \dfrac{1 \text{ ton}}{\boxed{} \text{ lb}}$

$10{,}000 \text{ lb} = \boxed{} \text{ tons}$

Think: pounds to tons — 1 ton =

$\boxed{}$ lb, so use $\dfrac{1 \text{ ton}}{\boxed{} \text{ lb}}$.

Multiply 10,000 lb by the conversion factor.

Cancel the common unit, $\boxed{}$.

Example 2

Convert 3 quarts to cups.

3 quarts = _____ cups

$\dfrac{4 \text{ c}}{1 \text{ qt}} = \dfrac{x \text{ c}}{3 \text{ qt}}$

1 quart is $\boxed{}$ cups. Write a proportion.

Use a $\boxed{}$ for the value you are trying to find.

$1 \cdot \boxed{} = 4 \cdot \boxed{}$

The cross products are equal.

$x = \boxed{}$

3 quarts = $\boxed{}$ cups

Copyright © by Holt McDougal.
All rights reserved.

Holt McDougal Mathematics

Example 3 PROBLEM SOLVING APPLICATION

The football goal posts are 30 feet tall. How many inches is this?

1. **Understand the Problem**

   The answer will be the [_____] of the goal posts in [_____].

   List the important information:

   • The height of the goal posts are 30 [_____].

2. **Make a Plan**

   Make a table from the information to show the number of [_____] in 1, 2, and 3 feet. Then find the number of inches in *n* feet.

3. **Solve**

Feet	Inches
1	[____]
2	[____]
3	[____]
n	[____]

   Look for a pattern.

   $1 \cdot 12 =$ [____]

   $2 \cdot 12 =$ [____]

   $3 \cdot 12 =$ [____]

   $n \cdot 12 =$ [____]

   30 · [____] = [_____] so the goal posts are [_____] inches tall.

4. **Look Back**

   Round 12 to 10. Then multiply by 30. 30 · 10 = 300
   The answer is reasonable because 360 is close to 300.

Check It Out!

1. Convert 15,840 feet to miles. [____]

2. Convert 144 cups to gallons. [____].

Copyright © by Holt McDougal.
All rights reserved.

Holt McDougal Mathematics

Converting Metric Units

Lesson Objectives

Convert metric units of measure

Additional Examples

Example 1

The high-jumper cleared a height of 1.75 m. How many centimeters is this height?

1.75 m = _____ cm

Think: Meter to centimeter is going

from a [_____] unit to a

[_____] unit. A centimeter is

[____] places to the right of meter in the

chart, so 10 · 10 or 10^2 = [_____].

1.75 m = (1.75 · [_____]) cm

1 m = [_____] cm. You are converting

a [_____] unit to a [_____]

unit, so [_____] by 100.

1.75 m = [_____] cm

Move the decimal point [____] places to the right.

Example 2

Convert.

A. The CD case is 14 cm wide. 14 cm = _____ m

14 cm = (14 ÷ [_____]) m

[_____] cm = [_____] m,

[_____] unit to [_____] unit; so

[_____] by [_____].

14 cm = [_____] m

Move the decimal point [____] places to

the [_____].

Copyright © by Holt McDougal.
All rights reserved.

Holt McDougal Mathematics

Example 3

Convert.

A. Method 1: Use a conversion factor.

16 m = _____ cm

Think: 1 m = $\boxed{}$ cm, so use

$\dfrac{\boxed{}\ cm}{1\ m}$.

16 m̸ × $\dfrac{\boxed{}\ cm}{1\ m̸}$ = $\boxed{}$ cm   Multiply by the conversion factor.

Cancel the common unit, $\boxed{}$.

B. Method 2: Use proportions.

450 g = _____ kg

$\dfrac{450\ g}{x\ kg} = \dfrac{1{,}000\ g}{1\ kg}$ Write a proportion.

1,000 $\boxed{}$ = $\boxed{}$ The cross products are equal.

x = $\boxed{}$ kg   Divide both sides by $\boxed{}$ to undo the multiplication.

Check It Out!

1. A farmer's barrel of corn has a mass of 15.5 kg. How much is this in grams?

2. The juice box contains 0.4 L.

0.4 L = _____ mL

3. Convert.

8,500 g = _____ kg

Copyright © by Holt McDougal.
All rights reserved.

Holt McDougal Mathematics

Time and Temperature

Lesson Objectives

Find measures of time and temperature

Additional Examples

Example 1

Convert.

A. 2 hr 5 min = _____ min

2 hours 5 minutes

[ ] minutes + 5 minutes   Think: 1 hour = [ ] minutes.

[ ] minutes

2 hr 5 min = [ ] min

B. 195 min = _____ hr

$195 \text{ min} \cdot \dfrac{1 \text{ hr}}{60 \text{ min}} = \dfrac{[\quad]}{[\quad]}$ hr   Think: 1 hour = [ ] minutes.

195 min = [ ] hr   Write as a mixed number.

Example 2

Solve each equation.

A. Shawn was scheduled to arrive at 10:15 A.M. He was 1 hour and 55 minutes late. When did he arrive?

Scheduled time: [ ] A.M.

Think: [ ] hour after 10:15 A.M.

is [ ] A.M. [ ] minutes

after 11:15 A.M. is [ ] P.M.

Arrival time: [ ]

Shawn arrived at [ ]

Copyright © by Holt McDougal.
All rights reserved.

Holt McDougal Mathematics

B. Ty met his friends at 1:35 P.M. He had traveled for 2 hours and 45 minutes.
   At what time did Ty begin his trip?

Meeting time: [____] P.M.   Think: [__] hours before 1:35 P.M.

                                    is [____] A.M. [__] minutes

                                    before 11:35 A.M. is [____] A.M.

Begin time: [_____]

Ty began his trip at [_____]

Example 3

Estimate the temperature.

40°C is about ____° F.

$F = \dfrac{9}{5} \cdot C + 32$ Use the formula.

Round $\dfrac{9}{5}$ to [__], and 32 to [__].

$F = 2 \cdot$ [____] $+ 30$ Use the order of operations.

$F =$ [____] $+ 30$

$F =$ [____]   40°C is about [____]° F.

Check It Out!

1. Convert.

   2 days = _____ min

[_____]

**2. Trent's ferry was scheduled to arrive at 9:45 A.M. It was 1 hour and
   15 minutes late. When did it arrive?**

[_____]

Copyright © by Holt McDougal.
All rights reserved.

Holt McDougal Mathematics

Finding Angle Measures in Polygons

Lesson Objectives

Find angle measures in polygons

Additional Examples

Example 1

Use the protractor to find the measure of ∠XYZ. Then classify the angle.

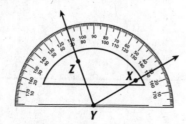

- Place the center point of the protractor on the ▭ of the angle.

- Read the measure where ray ▭ and ray ▭ cross.

- Ray *YX* crosses at ▭°, and ray *YZ* crosses at ▭°.

- The measure of ∠*XYZ* is ▭° – ▭°, or ▭°.

  Write this as m∠*XYZ* = ▭°.

- Since ▭° ≤ 90°, the angle is ▭.

Check

Use the other scale on the protractor to find the measure of ∠*XYZ*.

▭° – ▭° = ▭°

Copyright © by Holt McDougal.
All rights reserved.

Holt McDougal Mathematics

Example 2

Estimate the measure of ∠K in parallelogram *JKLM* below. Then use a protractor to check the reasonableness of your answer.

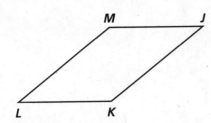

Think: The measure of the angle is close to

$135°$ ($90° +$ [ ]°), but it is a little more.

A good estimate would be about [ ]°.

Use the protractor.

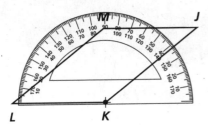

The measure of the angle is [ ]°.

m∠K = 142°, so the estimate of 145° is reasonable.

Example 3

A softball home plate is shown below. Find the measures of ∠C and ∠E.

Use a protractor to measure ∠C.

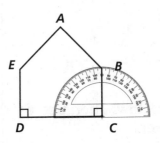

∠C = [ ]°

Copyright © by Holt McDougal.
All rights reserved.

Holt McDougal Mathematics

A softball home plate is shown below. Find the measures of ∠C and ∠E.

Estimate the m∠E.

It is greater than 90°, so it is [＿＿＿＿＿＿]. It looks as if the angle

measure is 90° + [＿＿＿]°.

So m ∠[＿＿] is about [＿＿＿＿]°.

Use a protractor to measure ∠E.

∠E = [＿＿＿]°

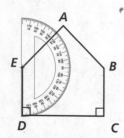

Check It Out!

1. **Use the protractor to find the measure of ∠LMN. Then classify the angle.**

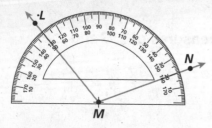

2. **Estimate the measure of ∠D in parallelogram *ABCD* below. Then use a protractor to check the reasonableness of your answer.**

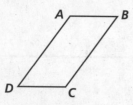

Copyright © by Holt McDougal.
All rights reserved.

Holt McDougal Mathematics

Perimeter

Lesson Objectives

Find the perimeter and missing side lengths of a polygon

Vocabulary

perimeter (p. 506) _____

_____

Additional Examples

Example 1

Find the perimeter of the figure.

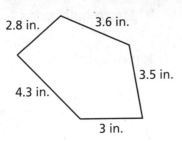

2.8 in. 3.6 in.
3.5 in.
4.3 in.
3 in.

[____] all the side lengths.

[____] + [____] + [____] + [____] + [____]

= [____]

The perimeter is [____] in.

Example 2

Find the perimeter *P* of the rectangle.

12 cm

3 cm

$P = 2l + 2w$

$P = (2 \cdot \boxed{}) + (2 \cdot \boxed{})$ Substitute $\boxed{}$ for *l* and $\boxed{}$ for *w*.

$P = \boxed{} + \boxed{}$ Multiply.

$P = \boxed{}$ Add.

The perimeter is [____] cm.

Copyright © by Holt McDougal.
All rights reserved.

Holt McDougal Mathematics

Example 3

Find the unknown measure.

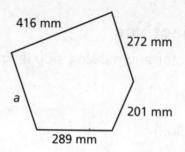

416 mm
272 mm
a
201 mm
289 mm

A. What is the length of side *a* if the perimeter equals 1,471 mm?

P = sum of side lengths

Use the values you know.

$1{,}471 = \boxed{} + \boxed{} + \boxed{} + \boxed{} + a$

$1{,}471 = \boxed{} + a$ Add the known lengths.

$1{,}471 - 1{,}178 = 1{,}178 + a - 1{,}178$ Subtract $\boxed{}$ from both sides.

$\boxed{} = a$ Side *a* is $\boxed{}$ mm long.

B. What is the perimeter of the polygon?

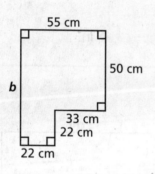

55 cm
50 cm
b
33 cm
22 cm
22 cm

First find the $\boxed{}$ side length.

Find the sides $\boxed{}$ side *b*.

The length of side

$b = \boxed{} + \boxed{}$.

Side *b* is $\boxed{}$ cm long.

$P = \boxed{} + \boxed{} + \boxed{} + \boxed{} + \boxed{} + \boxed{} = \boxed{}$

Find the perimeter.

The perimeter of the polygon is $\boxed{}$ cm.

Copyright © by Holt McDougal.
All rights reserved.

Holt McDougal Mathematics

C. The width of a rectangle is 19 cm. What is the perimeter of the rectangle if the length is 4 times the width?

4w

19 cm

$\ell = 4w$ Find the length.

$\ell = (4 \cdot \boxed{})$ Substitute $\boxed{}$ for w

$\ell = \boxed{}$

68

19 cm

$P = \boxed{}$ Use the formula for the perimeter of a rectangle.

$P = 2(\boxed{}) + 2(\boxed{})$ Substitute $\boxed{}$ and $\boxed{}$.

$P = \boxed{} + \boxed{}$ Multiply.

$P = \boxed{}$ Add.

The perimeter of the rectangle is $\boxed{}$ cm.

Check It Out!

1. Find the perimeter of the figure.

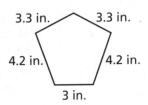

3.3 in.   3.3 in.

4.2 in.   4.2 in.

3 in.

2. Find the perimeter *P* of the rectangle.

15 cm

2 cm

Copyright © by Holt McDougal.
All rights reserved.

Holt McDougal Mathematics

Circles and Circumference

Lesson Objectives

Identify the parts of a circle and find the circumference of a circle

Vocabulary

circle (p. 512) _____

_____

center (p. 512) _____

_____

chord (p. 512) _____

_____

diameter (p. 512) _____

_____

radius (p. 512) _____

_____

circumference (p. 512) _____

_____

pi (p. 512) _____

_____

Additional Examples

Example 1

Name the circle, two chords, a diameter, and three radii.

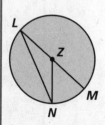

The circle is circle [ ].

[ ] is a diameter.

[ ] and [ ] are chords.

[ ], [ ], and [ ] are radii.

Copyright © by Holt McDougal.
All rights reserved.

Holt McDougal Mathematics

Example 2

A skydiver is laying out a circular target for his next jump. Estimate the circumference of the target by rounding π to 3.

8 ft

$C = \pi d$ Use the formula.

$C \approx \boxed{} \cdot \boxed{}$ Replace π with $\boxed{}$ and d with $\boxed{}$.

$C \approx \boxed{}$

The circumference of the circle is about $\boxed{}$ feet.

Example 3

Find the missing value to the nearest hundredth. Use 3.14 for *pi*.

A.

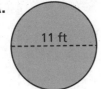
11 ft

$d = 11$ ft; $C = ?$

$C = \pi d$ Write the formula.

$C \approx \boxed{} \cdot \boxed{}$ Replace π with $\boxed{}$ and

                       d with $\boxed{}$.

$C \approx \boxed{}$ ft

B.

5 cm

$r = 5$ cm; $C = ?$

$C = 2\pi r$ Write the formula.

$C \approx 2 \cdot \boxed{} \cdot \boxed{}$ Replace π with $\boxed{}$ and

                       r with $\boxed{}$.

$C \approx \boxed{}$ cm

Copyright © by Holt McDougal.
All rights reserved.

Holt McDougal Mathematics

Check It Out!

1. Name the circle, two chords, a diameter, and three radii.

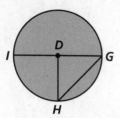

2. A second skydiver is laying out a circular target for his next jump. Estimate the circumference of the target by rounding π to 3.

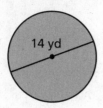

14 yd

3. Find the missing value of the nearest hundredth. Use 3.14 for *pi*.
   $C = 18.84$ cm; $d = ?$

Copyright © by Holt McDougal.
All rights reserved.

Holt McDougal Mathematics

9-1 Understanding Customary Units of Measure

What unit of measure provides the best estimate?

1. An ink pen is about 6 _____ long.

2. A horse weighs about 1,000 _____.

3. A small fish tank holds about 10 _____ of water.

9-2 Understanding Metric Units of Measure

What unit of measure provides the best estimate? Justify your answer.

4. The length of a screwdriver is about 20 _____.

5. The mass of a full soup can is 305 _____.

6. A baby bottle holds about 250 _____ of liquid.

9-3 Converting Customary Units

Convert.

7. 33 ft = _____ yd

8. 3 pt = _____ oz

9. 60 in. = _____ ft

10. 20,000 lb = _____ T

11. 7 lb = _____ oz

12. 192 oz = _____ gal

9-4 Converting Metric Units

13. A soda container holds 2 liters. How many milliliters of soda are in the container?

14. A juice glass holds 150 mL. 150 mL = _____ L.

15. The length of a driveway is 45 meters. 45 m = _____ km.

16. The mass of a brick is 1.5 kg. 1.5 kg = _____ g.

Copyright © by Holt McDougal.
All rights reserved.

Holt McDougal Mathematics

9-5 Time and Temperature

Convert.

17. 40 min = _____ s

18. 49 days = _____ weeks

19. 240 min = _____ h

20. 84 mo = _____ yr

21. A baseball game which began at 2:10 P.M. lasted 2 hours and 25 minutes. At what time was the game over?

Estimate the temperature.

22. 15°C is about _____°F.

23. 84°F is about _____°C.

9-6 Finding Angle Measures in Polygons

Estimate the measure of ∠A in each figure. Then use a protractor to check the reasonableness of your answer.

24.
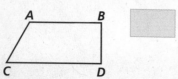

25.

26. The shape of a flower garden is shown below. Find the measure of ∠A and ∠B.

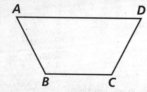

9-7 Perimeter

Find the perimeter of each figure.

27.
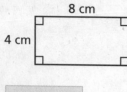
8 cm
4 cm

28.
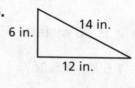
14 in.
6 in.
12 in.

Copyright © by Holt McDougal.
All rights reserved.

Holt McDougal Mathematics

Find the unknown measure.

29. What is the length of side *b* if the perimeter equals 50 ft?

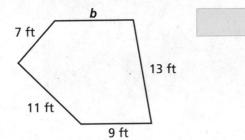

30. The width of a rectangle is 6 in. The perimeter of the rectangle is 30 in. What is the length of the rectangle?

9-8 Circles and Circumference

31. Point *Q* is the center of the circle. Name the circle, a diameter, and three radii.

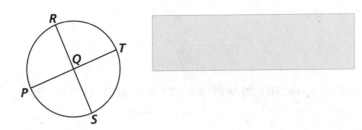

32. A landscaping company needs to dig a circular hole for planting a tree. If the diameter of the circular hole is 3 ft, what is its circumference? (Find the circumference by rounding π to 3).

Find each missing value to the nearest hundredth. Use 3.14 for π.

33. $r = 5$ cm; $C = $ _____.

34. $d = 12$ in.; $C = $ _____.

Copyright © by Holt McDougal.
All rights reserved.

Holt McDougal Mathematics

Answer these questions to summarize the important concepts from Chapter 9 in your own words.

1. Explain how to convert 108 inches to feet.

2. Explain how to convert 5 weeks to seconds.

3. Explain how to convert 70°F to °C using estimation.

4. Explain how to find the perimeter of a rectangle with length 4 ft and width 7 ft.

5. Explain how to find the circumference of a circle with radius 6 inches.

For more review of Chapter 9:

- Complete the Chapter 9 Study Guide and Review on pages 522–524 of your textbook.

- Complete the Ready to Go On quizzes on pages 500 and 518 of your textbook.

Copyright © by Holt McDougal.
All rights reserved.

Holt McDougal Mathematics

Area of Rectangles and Parallelograms

Lesson Objectives

Estimate the area of irregular figures and find the area of rectangles and parallelograms

Vocabulary

area (p. 534) _____

_____

Additional Examples

Example 1

Estimate the area of the figure.

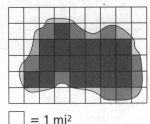

☐ = 1 mi²

Count full squares: ☐ squares.

Count almost-full squares: ☐ squares.

Count squares that are about half-full:

☐ half-full squares = ☐ full squares.

Do not count almost empty squares.

Add. ☐ + ☐ + ☐ = ☐

The area of the figure is about ☐ mi².

Example 2

Find the area of the rectangle.

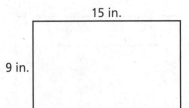

15 in.

9 in.

$A = lw$ Write the formula.

$A = $ ☐ · ☐   Substitute ☐ for l.

                 Substitute ☐ for w.

$A = $ ☐

The area is ☐ in².

Copyright © by Holt McDougal.
All rights reserved.

Holt McDougal Mathematics

Example 3

Find the area of the parallelogram.

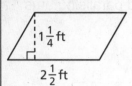

$1\frac{1}{4}$ ft

$2\frac{1}{2}$ ft

$A = bh$ Write the formula.

$A = \boxed{} \cdot \boxed{}$ Substitute $\boxed{}$ for b and $\boxed{}$ for h.

$A = \boxed{} \cdot \boxed{}$ Multiply.

$A = \boxed{}$ or $\boxed{}$

The area is $\boxed{}$ ft².

Example 4

Jessika is going to tile a kitchen that measures 13 ft by 17 ft. Some floor space is taken up by an island that measures 3 ft by 6 ft. How much area remains to be tiled in the kitchen?

To find the area of the kitchen that remains, $\boxed{}$ the area

of the $\boxed{}$ from the area of the $\boxed{}$.

kitchen area	−	island area	=	kitchen area remaining
$(13 \cdot 17)$	−	$(3 \cdot 6)$	=	n
$\boxed{}$	−	$\boxed{}$	=	$\boxed{}$

The area of the kitchen that remains is $\boxed{}$ ft².

Check It Out!

1. Estimate the area of the figure.

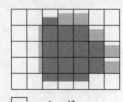

$\square$ = 1 mi²

Copyright © by Holt McDougal.
All rights reserved.

Holt McDougal Mathematics

Area of Triangles and Trapezoids

Lesson Objectives

Find the area of triangles and trapezoids

Additional Examples

Example 1

Find the area of each triangle.

A.

$A = \frac{1}{2}bh$ .... Write the formula.

$A = \frac{1}{2}(\boxed{} \cdot \boxed{})$ .... Substitute $\boxed{}$ for b.

Substitute $\boxed{}$ for h.

$A = \frac{1}{2}(\boxed{})$ .... Multiply.

$A = \boxed{}$

The area is $\boxed{}$ ft^2.

Example 2

The diagram shows the section of a forest being studied. What is the area of the section?

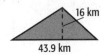

$A = \frac{1}{2}bh$ .... Write the formula.

$A = \frac{1}{2}(\boxed{} \cdot \boxed{})$ .... Substitute $\boxed{}$ for b. Substitute

$\boxed{}$ for h.

$A = \frac{1}{2}(\boxed{}) = \boxed{}$ .... Multiply.

The area of the forest being studied is $\boxed{}$ ft^2.

Copyright © by Holt McDougal.
All rights reserved.
Holt McDougal Mathematics

Example 3

Find the area of the trapezoid.

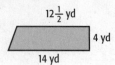

$A = \frac{1}{2}h(b_1 + b_2)$ Write the formula.

$A = \frac{1}{2}(\boxed{})(\boxed{} + \boxed{})$ Substitute $\boxed{}$ for h, $\boxed{}$ for b_1

and $\boxed{}$ for b_2.

$A = \frac{1}{2}(4)(\boxed{}) = \boxed{}$ Multiply.

The area is $\boxed{}$ yd^2.

Check It Out!

1. Find the area of the triangle.

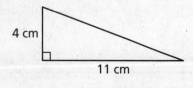

2. The diagram shows the floor plan for a triangular dining area. What is the area of the floor?

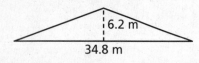

Copyright © by Holt McDougal.
All rights reserved.

     Holt McDougal Mathematics

Area of Composite Figures

Lesson Objectives

Break a polygon into simpler parts to find its area

Additional Examples

Example 1

Find the area of each polygon.

A.

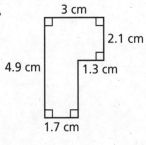

3 cm

2.1 cm

4.9 cm   1.3 cm

1.7 cm

Think: Break the polygon apart into [_____].

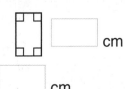

[____] cm

[____] cm

[____] cm

[____] cm

Find the area of each rectangle.

$A = lw$ $A = lw$ Write the formula for the area of a

[_____].

$A =$ [____] · [____] $A =$ [____] · [____]

$A =$ [____] $A =$ [____]

[____] + [____] = [_____]   [____] to find the total area.

The area of the polygon is [_____] cm².

Copyright © by Holt McDougal.
All rights reserved.

Holt McDougal Mathematics

Example 2

Patrick made a design. Use the coordinate grid to find its area.

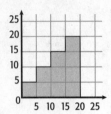

Think: Divide the design into ☐ rectangles.

Find the area of each rectangle.

Rectangle 1

$l =$ ☐, $w =$ ☐; $A =$ ☐ · ☐ = ☐

Rectangle 2

$l =$ ☐, $w =$ ☐; $A =$ ☐ · ☐ = ☐

Rectangle 3

$l =$ ☐, $w =$ ☐; $A =$ ☐ · ☐ = ☐

Rectangle 4

$l =$ ☐, $w =$ ☐; $A =$ ☐ · ☐ = ☐

Add the area of the rectangles to find the total area of the figure.

☐ + ☐ + ☐ + ☐ = ☐ square units

The area of the design is ☐ square units.

Check It Out!

1. Find the area of the polygon.

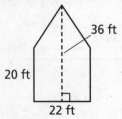

36 ft

20 ft

22 ft

Copyright © by Holt McDougal.
All rights reserved.
Holt McDougal Mathematics

Changing Dimensions

Lesson Objectives

Make a model to explore how area and perimeter are affected by changes in the dimensions of a figure

Additional Examples

Example 1

Find how the perimeter and area of the figure change when its dimensions change.

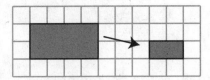

Divide each dimension by 2.

$P =$ ☐ units $P =$ ☐ units

$A =$ ☐ square units $A =$ ☐ square units

When the dimensions of the rectangle are divided by 2, the perimeter is

divided by ☐, and the area is divided by ☐.

Copyright © by Holt McDougal.
All rights reserved.

Holt McDougal Mathematics

Example 2

Draw a rectangle whose dimensions are 4 times as large as the given rectangle. How do the perimeter and area change?

3 cm

2 cm [ ] ⟶   Multiply each dimension by 4.

$P =$ [ ] cm $P =$ [ ] cm

$A =$ [ ] cm² $A =$ [ ] cm²

When the dimensions of the rectangle are multiplied by 4, the perimeter is

multiplied by [ ], and the area is multiplied by [ ], or [ ].

Check It Out!

1. Find how the perimeter and area of the figure change when its dimensions change.

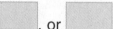

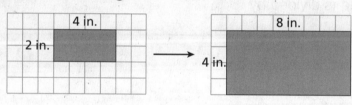

2. Draw a rectangle whose dimensions are 2 times as large as the given rectangle. How do the perimeter and area change?

5 cm

3 cm [ ]

Copyright © by Holt McDougal.
All rights reserved.

Holt McDougal Mathematics

Area of Circles

Lesson Objectives

Find the area of a circle

Additional Examples

Example 1

Estimate the area of the circle. Use 3 to approximate π.

A.

19.7 m

$A = \pi r^2$ — Write the formula for the area.

$A \approx \boxed{} \cdot \boxed{}^2$ — Replace π with 3 and r with $\boxed{}$.

$A \approx 3 \cdot \boxed{}$ — Use the order of operations.

$A \approx \boxed{}$

B.

28 ft

$A = \pi r^2$ — Write the formula for the area.

$r = d \div 2$

$r = \boxed{} \div 2 = \boxed{}$ — The length of the radius is $\boxed{}$ the length of the diameter.

$A \approx 3 \cdot \boxed{}^2$ — Replace π with 3 and r with $\boxed{}$.

$A \approx 3 \cdot \boxed{}$ — Use the order of operations.

$A \approx \boxed{}$ ft^2 — Multiply.

Copyright © by Holt McDougal.
All rights reserved.

Holt McDougal Mathematics

Example 2

Find the area of the circle. Use $\frac{22}{7}$ for π.

A.

$A = \pi r^2$ · Write the formula for the area.

$r = \boxed{} \div 2$ · The length of the $\boxed{}$ is half the length

$r = \boxed{} \div 2 = \boxed{}$ · of the $\boxed{}$.

$A \approx \frac{22}{7} \cdot \boxed{}^2$ · Replace π with $\frac{22}{7}$ and r with $\boxed{}$.

$A \approx \frac{22}{7} \cdot \boxed{}$ · Simplify.

$A \approx \boxed{}$ ft^2

Example 3

A drum head has a radius of 18 in. Find the area of the material covering the drum head. Use 3.14 for π.

$A = \pi r^2$ · Write the formula for the area.

$A \approx 3.14 \cdot \boxed{}^2$ · Replace π with 3.14 and r with $\boxed{}$.

$A \approx 3.14 \cdot \boxed{}$ · Simplify.

$A \approx \boxed{}$

Check It Out!

1. Estimate the area of the circle. Use 3 to approximate π.

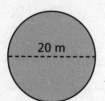

Copyright © by Holt McDougal.
All rights reserved.

Holt McDougal Mathematics

Three-Dimensional Figures

Lesson Objectives

Name three-dimensional figures

Vocabulary

polyhedron (p. 560) _____

_____

face (p. 560) _____

_____

edge (p. 560) _____

_____

vertex (p. 560) _____

_____

prism (p. 560) _____

_____

base (p. 560) _____

_____

cylinder (p. 560) _____

_____

pyramid (p. 561) _____

_____

cone (p. 561) _____

_____

sphere (p. 561) _____

_____

Copyright © by Holt McDougal.
All rights reserved.

Holt McDougal Mathematics

Additional Examples

Example 1

Identify the number of faces, edges, and vertices on each three-dimensional figure.

A.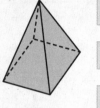

⬜ faces

⬜ edges

⬜ vertices

B.

⬜ faces

⬜ edges

⬜ vertices

Example 2

Name the three-dimensional figure represented by each object.

A.

There is a ⬜ surface.

The figure is not a ⬜.

There are two ⬜,

⬜ bases.

The bases are ⬜.

The figure represents a ⬜.

Check It Out!

1. Identify the number of faces, edges, and vertices on the three-dimensional figure.

Copyright © by Holt McDougal.
All rights reserved.

Holt McDougal Mathematics

Volume of Prisms

Lesson Objectives

Estimate and find the volumes of rectangular prisms and triangular prisms

Vocabulary

volume (p. 566) _____

_____

Additional Examples

Example 1

Find the volume of the rectangular prism.

13 in.

26 in.   11 in.

$V = lwh$ Write the formula.

$V = \boxed{} \cdot \boxed{} \cdot \boxed{}$ $l = \boxed{}$; $w = \boxed{}$; $h = \boxed{}$

$V = \boxed{}$ in^3 Multiply.

Example 2

Find the volume of each triangular prism.

A.

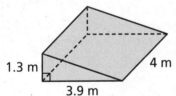

1.3 m   4 m

3.9 m

$V = Bh$ Write the formula.

$V = \left(\frac{1}{2} \cdot \boxed{} \cdot \boxed{} \right) \cdot \boxed{}$ $B = \frac{1}{2} \cdot \boxed{} \cdot \boxed{}$; $h = \boxed{}$

$V = \boxed{}$ m^3 Multiply.

Copyright © by Holt McDougal.
All rights reserved.

Holt McDougal Mathematics

Example 3 PROBLEM SOLVING APPLICATION

Suppose a facial tissue company ships 16 cubic tissue boxes in each case. What are the possible dimensions for a case of tissue boxes?

1. Understand the Problem

The answer will be all possible dimensions for a case of 16 cubic boxes. List the important information:

- There are [   ] tissue boxes in a case.

- The boxes are [   ], or [   ] prisms.

2. Make a Plan

You can make [   ] using cubes to find the possible

[   ] for a case of 16 tissue boxes.

3. Solve

You can make models using cubes to find the possible dimensions for a case of 16 cubes.

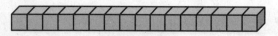

The possible dimensions for a case of 16 cubic tissue boxes are:

[   ] · [   ] · [   ], [   ] · [   ] · [   ], [   ] · [   ] · [   ], [   ] · [   ] · [   ]

4. Look Back

Each dimension is a factor of 16. The product of the dimensions (length · width · height) is 16, so the volume of each case is 16 cubes.

Check It Out!

1. Find the volume of the rectangular prism.

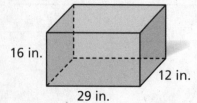

16 in.
12 in.
29 in.

Copyright © by Holt McDougal.
All rights reserved.

Holt McDougal Mathematics

Volume of Cylinders

Lesson Objectives

Find volumes of cylinders

Additional Examples

Example 1

Find the volume V of the cylinder to the nearest cubic unit.

A. $r = 4$ ft; $h = 7$ ft

$r = 4$ ft

$h = 7$ ft

$V = \pi r^2 h$

$V = \boxed{} \times \boxed{}^2 \times \boxed{}$ Replace π with $\boxed{}$, r with $\boxed{}$,

and h with $\boxed{}$.

$V = \boxed{}$ Multiply.

The volume is about $\boxed{}$ ft³.

Example 2

Ali has a cylinder-shaped pencil holder with a 3-in. diameter and a height of 5 in. Scott has a cylinder-shape pencil holder with a 4-in. diameter and a height of 6 in. Estimate the volume of each cylinder holder to the nearest cubic inch.

A. Ali's pencil holder

3 in. ÷ 2 = 1.5 in.   Find the radius.

$V = \pi r^2 h$ Write the formula.

$V = \boxed{} \times \boxed{}^2 \times \boxed{}$ Replace π with $\boxed{}$, r with

$\boxed{}$, and h with $\boxed{}$.

$V = \boxed{}$ Multiply.

The volume of Ali's pencil holder is about 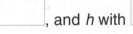 in³.

Copyright © by Holt McDougal.
All rights reserved.

 **Holt McDougal Mathematics**

Example 3

Find which cylinder has the greater volume.

Cylinder 1:

$V = \boxed{} \times \boxed{}^2 \times \boxed{}$

$V = \boxed{}$ cm³

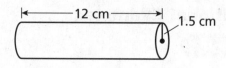

Cylinder 2:

$V = \boxed{} \times \boxed{}^2 \times \boxed{}$

$V = \boxed{}$ cm³

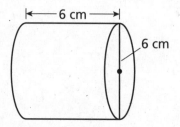

Cylinder 2 has the greater volume because $\boxed{}$ cm³ > $\boxed{}$ cm³.

Check It Out!

1. Find the volume V of the cylinder to the nearest cubic unit.

   $r = 6$ ft; $h = 5$ ft

2. Julie built a cylinder-shaped tower with a 12-yd diameter and a height of 8 yd. Estimate the volume of Julie's tower to the nearest cubic yard.

3. Find which cylinder has the greater volume.

   Cylinder 1: 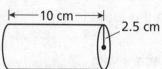   Cylinder 2: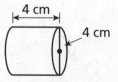

Copyright © by Holt McDougal.
All rights reserved.

Holt McDougal Mathematics

Surface Area

Lesson Objectives

Find the surface areas of prisms, pyramids, and cylinders

Vocabulary

surface area (p. 576) _____

_____

net (p. 576) _____

_____

Additional Examples

Example 1

Find the surface area *S* of the prism.

A. Method 1: Use a net.

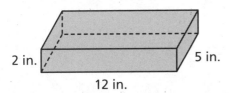

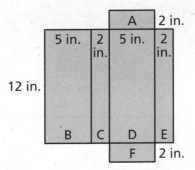

Draw a [　　　] to help you see each [　　　　　] of the prism.

Use the formula [　　　　] to find the area of each face.

A: $A =$ [　] $\times$ [　] $=$ [　　]　　　D: $A =$ [　] $\times$ [　] $=$ [　　]

B: $A =$ [　] $\times$ [　] $=$ [　　]　　　E: $A =$ [　] $\times$ [　] $=$ [　　]

C: $A =$ [　] $\times$ [　] $=$ [　　]　　　F: $A =$ [　] $\times$ [　] $=$ [　　]

[　　　] the areas of each face.

$S =$ [　] $+$ [　] $+$ [　] $+$ [　] $+$ [　] $+$ [　] $=$ [　　] in²

The surface area is [　　　] in².

Copyright © by Holt McDougal.
All rights reserved.

Holt McDougal Mathematics

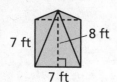

Example 2

Find the surface area *S* of the pyramid.

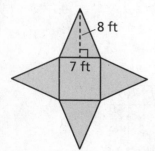

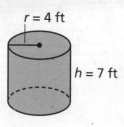

$S =$ area of ⬚ $+ 4 \times$ (area of ⬚ face)

$S = s^2 + 4 \times \left(\frac{1}{2}bh\right)$

$S = \square^2 + 4 \times \left(\frac{1}{2} \times 7 \times 8\right)$ Substitute.

$S = \square + 4 \times \square$

$S = \square + \square$

$S = $ ▨

The surface area is ▨ ft².

Example 3

Find the surface area *S* of the cylinder. Use 3.14 for π, and round to the nearest hundredth.

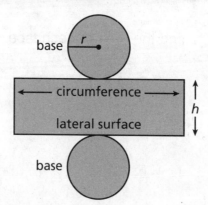

$S = $ area of ⬚ surface $+ 2 \times$ (area of each ⬚)

Copyright © by Holt McDougal.
All rights reserved.

Holt McDougal Mathematics

$S = h \times (2\pi r) + 2 \times (\pi r^2)$ Substitute.

$S = \boxed{} \times (2 \times \pi \times \boxed{}) + 2 \times (\pi \times \boxed{}^2)$

$S = \boxed{} \times \boxed{} \pi + 2 \times \boxed{} \pi$

$S \approx 7 \times 8(\underline{}) + 2 \times 16(\underline{})$ Use 3.14 for π.

$S \approx 7 \times 25.12 + 2 \times 50.24$

$S \approx \boxed{} + \boxed{}$

$S \approx \boxed{}$

The surface area is about $\boxed{}$ ft^2.

Check It Out!

1. Find the surface area S of the prism.

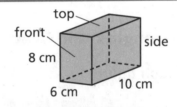

top, front, side
8 cm
6 cm
10 cm

2. Find the surface area S of the pyramid.

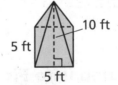

10 ft
5 ft
5 ft

3. Find the surface area S of the cylinder. Use 3.14 for π, and round to the nearest hundredth.

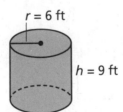

$r = 6$ ft
$h = 9$ ft

Copyright © by Holt McDougal.
All rights reserved.

Holt McDougal Mathematics

10-1 Area of Rectangles and Parallelograms

Find the area of each parallelogram.

1.

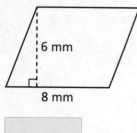

6 mm

8 mm

2.

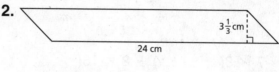

$3\frac{1}{3}$ cm

24 cm

3. Trisha has a rectangular garden with a walkway around it. The garden is 15 ft by 12 ft. Find the area of the walkway.

20 ft

15 ft

10-2 Area of Triangles and Trapezoids

Find the area of each figure.

3.

8 in.

6 in.

14 in.

4.

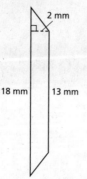

2 mm

18 mm   13 mm

10-3 Area of Composite Figures

Find the area of each polygon.

5.

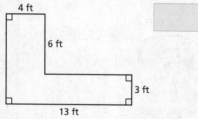

4 ft

6 ft

3 ft

13 ft

6.

15 cm

9 cm

5 cm

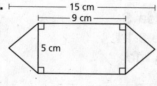

Copyright © by Holt McDougal.
All rights reserved.

Holt McDougal Mathematics

10-4 Changing Dimensions

7. Find how the perimeter and area of the rectangle change when its dimensions are multiplied by 5.

8. The dimensions of a triangle drawn on an overhead are 3 times larger when it is projected on the screen. Find the area of the new triangle if the original triangle is shown below.

4 cm

10 cm

10-5 Area of Circles

Find the area and circumference of each circle. Use 3.14 for *pi* and round to the nearest hundredth.

9.

18 ft

10.

4 cm

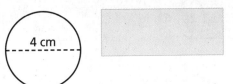

10-6 Three-Dimensional Figures

Identify the number of faces, edges, and vertices in each three-dimensional figure. Then name the figure and tell whether it is a polyhedron.

11.

12.

13.

Copyright © by Holt McDougal.
All rights reserved.

Holt McDougal Mathematics

10-7 Volume of Prisms

Find the volume of each figure.

14.
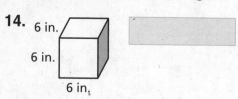

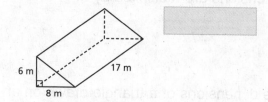

15. A book company packs 16 cubic boxes of books in a case. What are all the possible dimensions for a case of books?
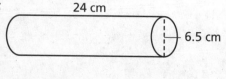

10-8 Volume of Cylinders

Find the volume of each cylinder to the nearest cubic unit.

16.
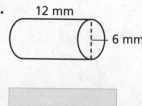

17.
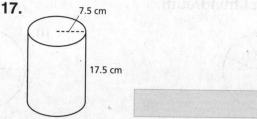

18. Soup is sold in a cylindrical container with a diameter of 8 cm and a height of 12 cm. Estimate the volume of the soup container to the nearest cubic cm.

10-9 Surface Area

Find the surface area of each figure. Use 3.14 for *pi* and round to the nearest hundredth.

19.

24 cm

6.5 cm

20.
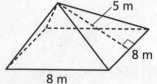

5 m

8 m

8 m

Copyright © by Holt McDougal.
All rights reserved.

Holt McDougal Mathematics

Big Ideas

Answer these questions to summarize the important concepts from Chapter 10 in your own words.

1. Explain how to find the area of a triangle with base 13 inches and height 12 inches.

2. Explain how to find the area of a composite figure.

3. Explain how the perimeter and area of a square change when its dimensions are doubled.

4. Explain how to find the volume of a cylinder with diameter 14 centimeters and height 18 centimeters.

5. Explain how to find the surface area of a square pyramid with base measurements of 5 feet and lateral height 7 feet.

For more review of Chapter 10:

- Complete the Chapter 10 Study Guide and Review on pages 584–586.
- Complete the Ready to Go On quizzes on pages 556 and 580.

Copyright © by Holt McDougal.
All rights reserved.

Holt McDougal Mathematics

Integers and Absolute Value

Lesson Objectives

Identify and graph integers, and find opposites

Vocabulary

positive number (p. 594) _____

negative number (p. 594) _____

opposites (p. 594) _____

_____

integers (p. 594) _____

absolute value (p. 595) _____

Additional Examples

Example 1

Name a positive or negative number to represent each situation.

A. a jet climbing to an altitude of 20,000 feet

[   ] numbers can represent climbing or rising.

[   ]

Example 2

Graph the integer and its opposite on a number line.

A. +2

[   ] is the same [   ] from 0 as +2.

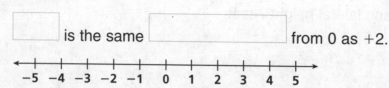

Copyright © by Holt McDougal.
All rights reserved.

Holt McDougal Mathematics

Example 3

Use a number line to find the absolute value of each integer.

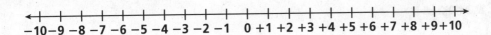

$$-10\ -9\ -8\ -7\ -6\ -5\ -4\ -3\ -2\ -1\quad 0\ +1\ +2\ +3\ +4\ +5\ +6\ +7\ +8\ +9\ +10$$

A. $|-2|$

⬜ -2 is ⬜ units from 0, so $|-2|$ is ⬜.

B. $|8|$

⬜ 8 is ⬜ units from 0, so $|8|$ is ⬜.

Check It Out!

1. Name a positive or negative number to represent the situation.

300 feet below sea level

2. Graph -4 and its opposite on a number line.

3. Use a number line to find the absolute value of the integer.

$|-9|$

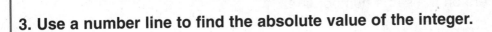

$$-10\ -9\ -8\ -7\ -6\ -5\ -4\ -3\ -2\ -1\quad 0\ +1\ +2\ +3\ +4\ +5\ +6\ +7\ +8\ +9\ +10$$

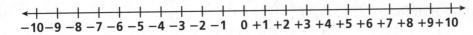

Copyright © by Holt McDougal.
All rights reserved.

Holt McDougal Mathematics

Comparing and Ordering Integers

Lesson Objectives

Compare and order integers

Additional Examples

Example 1

Use the number line to compare each pair of integers. Write < or >.

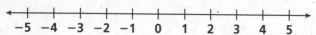

A. −2 ■ 2

−2 ▢ 2   −2 is to the ▢ of 2 on the number line.

B. 3 ■ −5

3 ▢ −5   3 is to the ▢ of −5 on the number line.

C. −1 ■ −4

−1 ▢ −4   −1 is to the ▢ of −4 on the number line.

Example 2

Order the integers in each set from least to greatest.

A. −2, 3, −1

Graph the integers on the same number line.

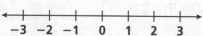

Then read the numbers from left to right: ▢, ▢, ▢.

B. 4, −3, −5, 2

Graph the integers on the same number line.

Then read the numbers from left to right: ▢, ▢, ▢, ▢.

Copyright © by Holt McDougal.
All rights reserved.

Holt McDougal Mathematics

Example 3 PROBLEM SOLVING APPLICATION

In a golf match, Craig scored +2, Cameron scored +3, and Rob scored −1. Who won the golf match?

1. **Understand the Problem**
   The answer will be the player with the [____] score.

   List the important information:

   • Craig scored [____].

   • Cameron scored [____].

   • Rob scored [____].

2. **Make a Plan**
   You can draw a diagram to order the scores from [____] to [____].

3. **Solve**
   Draw a number line and graph each player's score on it.

   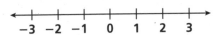

   Rob's score, [____], is farthest to the [____], so it is the [____] score. [____] won the golf match.

4. **Look Back**
   Negative integers are always less than positive integers, so neither Craig nor Cameron won the golf match.

Check It Out!

1. **Use the number line to compare each pair of integers. Write < or >.**

   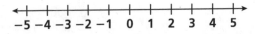

   2 ■ −3

Copyright © by Holt McDougal.
All rights reserved.

Holt McDougal Mathematics

The Coordinate Plane

Lesson Objectives

Locate and graph points on the coordinate plane

Vocabulary

coordinate plane (p. 604) _____

_____

axes (p. 604) _____

_____

x-axis (p. 604) _____

_____

y-axis (p. 604) _____

_____

quadrants (p. 604) _____

_____

origin (p. 604) _____

_____

coordinates (p. 604) _____

_____

x-coordinate (p. 604) _____

_____

y-coordinate (p. 604) _____

_____

Additional Examples

Example 1

Name the quadrant where
each point is located.

A. *X*

Quadrant [   ]

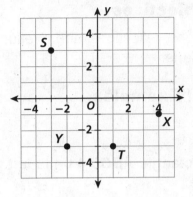

Example 2

Use the graph in Additional Example 1. Give the coordinates of each point.

A. *X*

From the origin, *X* is [   ] units right and [   ] unit down. ([   ])

Graph each point on a coordinate plane.

A. *V*(4, 2)

From the origin, move [   ] units

[   ] , and [   ] units [   ] .

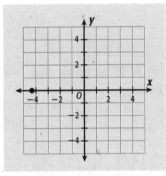

Check It Out!

1. Use the graph from Example 1. Name the quadrant where the point is located.

   T

   [   ]

Copyright © by Holt McDougal.
All rights reserved.

Holt McDougal Mathematics

Transformations in the Coordinate Plane

Lesson Objectives

Use translations, reflections, and rotations to change the position of figures in the coordinate plane.

Additional Examples

Example 1

Translate rectangle *ABCD* 4 units left. Give the coordinates of each vertex in the image.

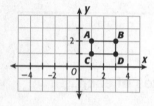

Each vertex is translated [ ] units left.

The vertices of the image are *A'* [ ], *B'* [ ], *C'* [ ],

and *D'* [ ].

Example 2

Reflect triangle *RST* across the *y*-axis. Give the coordinates of each vertex in the image.

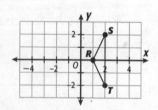

Each vertex of the image is the same distance from the [ ] as the corresponding vertex in the original figure.

The vertices of the image are *R'* [ ], *S'* [ ], and *T'* [ ].

Copyright © by Holt McDougal.
All rights reserved.

Holt McDougal Mathematics

Example 3

Rotate triangle *JKL* 90° counterclockwise about the origin. Give the coordinates of each vertex in the image.

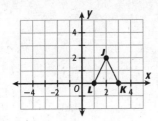

Notice that the vertex *K* is 3 units ▭ of the origin, and vertex *K'* is

3 units ▭ the origin.

The vertices of the image are *J'* ▭ , *K'* ▭ , and

L' ▭ .

Check It Out!

1. Translate square *ABCD* 6 units right. Give the coordinates of each vertex in the image.

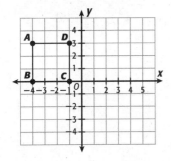

Adding Integers

Lesson Objectives

Add integers

Additional Examples

Example 1

Write the addition modeled on each number line.

A.

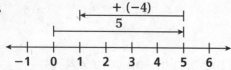

The addition modeled is ▢ + (▢) = ▢ .

B.

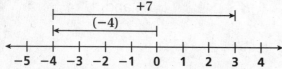

The addition modeled is ▢ + ▢ = ▢ .

C.

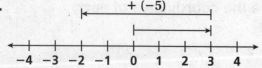

The addition modeled is ▢ + (▢) = ▢ .

Example 2

Find each sum.

A. $-3 + (-2)$ **B.** $6 + (-8)$

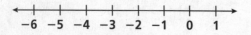 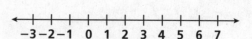

$-3 + (-2) =$ ▢ $6 + (-8) =$ ▢

Copyright © by Holt McDougal.
All rights reserved.

Holt McDougal Mathematics

Example 3

Evaluate $y + (-2)$ for $y = 7$.

$y + (-2)$ Write the expression.

$\boxed{} + (-2)$ Substitute $\boxed{}$ for y.

$\boxed{}$ Add.

Example 4

A sunken ship is 12 m below sea level. A search plane flies 35 m above the sunken ship. How far above the sea is the plane?

The ship is $\boxed{}$ m below the sea level and the plane is $\boxed{}$ m above the ship.

$\boxed{} + \boxed{}$

$\boxed{}$

The plane is $\boxed{}$ m above the sea.

Check It Out!

1. Write the addition modeled on the number line.

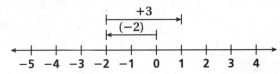

2. Find the sum.

$-2 + (-4)$

3. Evaluate $z + (-4)$ for $z = 2$.

Copyright © by Holt McDougal.
All rights reserved.
Holt McDougal Mathematics

Subtracting Integers

Lesson Objectives

Subtract integers

Additional Examples

Example 1

Write the subtraction modeled on each number line.

A.

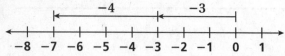

The subtraction modeled is [ ] − [ ] = [ ].

Example 2

Find each difference.

A. 4 − 6

B. 3 − (−3)

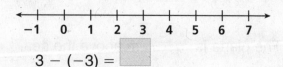

3 − (−3) = [ ]

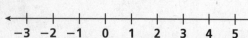

4 − 6 = [ ]

Example 3

Evaluate $a - 4$ for $a = 2$.

$a - 4$ Write the expression.

[ ] − 4 = [ ]   Substitute [ ] for a and subtract.

Check It Out!

1. Find the difference: 2 − (−5) [ ]

Copyright © by Holt McDougal.
All rights reserved.

Holt McDougal Mathematics

Multiplying Integers

Lesson Objectives

Multiply integers

Additional Examples

Example 1

Find each product.

A. 5 · 2

   5 · 2 = ☐   Think: 5 groups of ☐.

B. 4 · (−5)

   4 · (−5) = ☐   Think: 4 groups of ☐.

Example 2

Evaluate −7x for each value of x.

A. x = −3

   −7x   Write the expression.

   −7 · (☐)   Substitute ☐ for x.

  ☐   The signs are the ☐, so the answer is

  ☐.

Check It Out!

1. Find the product. −5 · 3 ☐

2. Evaluate −4y for y = −2 ☐

Copyright © by Holt McDougal.
All rights reserved.

Holt McDougal Mathematics

Dividing Integers

Lesson Objectives

Divide integers

Additional Examples

Example 1

Find each quotient.

A. $-30 \div 6$

Think: What number times [ ] equals -30?

[ ] $\cdot 6 = -30$, so $-30 \div 6 =$ [ ].

B. $-42 \div (-7)$

Think: What number times [ ] equals -42?

[ ] $\cdot (-7) = -42$, so $-42 \div (-7) =$ [ ].

Example 2

Evaluate $\frac{d}{4}$ for each value of d.

A. $d = 16$

$\frac{d}{4}$ Write the expression.

[ ] $=$ [ ] $\div 4$ Substitute [ ] for d.

The signs are the [ ], so the answer is

$=$ [ ]   [ ].

Check It Out!

1. Find the quotient. $-36 \div (-6)$ [ ]

2. Evaluate $\frac{c}{3}$ for $c = -15$ [ ]

Copyright © by Holt McDougal.
All rights reserved.

Holt McDougal Mathematics

Solving Integer Equations

Lesson Objectives

Solve equations containing integers

Additional Examples

Example 1

A. Solve $-8 + y = -13$.

$-8 + y = -13$ -8 is added to y.

$\underline{+8} \qquad \underline{+8}$ Subtracting ☐ from both sides to undo

$y = $ ☐   the ☐ is the same as

adding ☐.

B. Solve $n - 2 = -8$.

$n - 2 = -8$ 2 is subtracted from n.

$\underline{+2} \quad \underline{+2}$ Add ☐ to both sides to undo the

$n = $ ☐   ☐.

Example 2

Solve each equation. Check your answer.

A. $4m = -20$

$\dfrac{4m}{4} = \dfrac{-20}{4}$ m is multiplied by 4. ☐ both sides by

☐ to undo the ☐.

$m = $ ☐

Check It Out!

1. Solve $-2 + y = -7$. Check your answer.

Copyright © by Holt McDougal.
All rights reserved.

Holt McDougal Mathematics

CHAPTER 11

Chapter Review

11-1 Integers and Absolute Value

Name a positive or negative number to represent the situation.

1. a withdrawal of $50

Find each absolute value.

2. $|-3|$　　　**3.** $|16|$　　　**4.** $|0|$　　　**5.** $|-18|$

11-2 Comparing and Ordering Integers

6. Use the table, which shows a part of Beth's checking account statement.

   a. Which day did Beth have the highest balance in her checking account?

   b. Which day did Beth have the smallest balance in her checking account?

Date	Balance
May 1	$125.08
May 4	$205.67
May 11	$−15.32

Use the number line to compare each pair of integers. Write < or >.

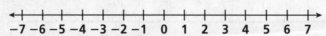

7. 0 ■ 5　　　**8.** 3 ■ −3　　　**9.** −6 ■ 4　　　**10.** 1 ■ −2

11-3 The Coordinate Plane

Name the quadrant where each ordered pair is located.

11. $(-3, 5)$　　　**12.** $(4, -2)$　　　**13.** $(-1\frac{1}{3}, -6)$　　　**14.** $(2, 8)$

15. Graph points $A(-3, -3)$, $B(3, -3)$, $C(2, 2)$, and $D(-4, 2)$. Connect the points. What type of quadrilateral do the points form?

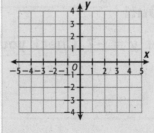

Copyright © by Holt McDougal.
All rights reserved.

Holt McDougal Mathematics

11-4 Transformations in the Coordinate Plane

Use the figure for Questions 16–18.

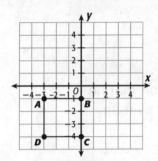

16. Translate figure *ABCD* 2 units up. Give the coordinates of each vertex in the image.

17. Reflect figure *ABCD* across the *y*-axis. Give the coordinates of each vertex in the image.

18. Rotate figure *ABCD* 90° counterclockwise about the origin. Give the coordinates of each vertex in the image.

11-5 Adding Integers

Evaluate each expression for the given value of the variable.

19. $x + (-6)$; $x = 8$ **20.** $n + (-4)$; $n = -9$ **21.** $-7 + r$; $r = 6$

22. Madison was playing a trivia game. She answered her first three 100-point questions incorrectly, and then answered a 500-point question correctly. How many points did she have after answering the 4 questions?

11-6 Subtracting Integers

Find each difference.

23. $9 - (-6)$ **24.** $-4 - 8$ **25.** $-10 - (-7)$ **26.** $4 - (-6)$

27. One December day in Breckenridge, Colorado, the high temperature was 24°F and the low temperature was −18°F. Find the difference between the high and low temperatures.

Copyright © by Holt McDougal.
All rights reserved.

Holt McDougal Mathematics

11-7 Multiplying Integers

Evaluate each expression for the given value of the variable.

28. $n \cdot (-5)$; $n = -4$

29. $-6 \cdot m$; $m = 7$

30. $14b$; $b = -8$

31. While playing a game, Tom scored -20 points for each question that he answered incorrectly. Tom answered 7 questions incorrectly. How many points did Tom score for those 7 questions?

11-8 Dividing Integers

Divide.

32. $-8 \div 4$

33. $\dfrac{30}{-6}$

34. $-49 \div (-7)$

35. $\dfrac{-81}{-9}$

36. The low temperature in Chicago was $-4°F$ on Friday, $-8°F$ on Saturday, and $3°F$ on Sunday. What was the average low temperature over the 3 days?

11-9 Solving Integer Equations

Solve each equation. Check your answers.

37. $y - 9 = 5$

38. $-8j = -72$

39. $b \div 6 = -9$

40. $25 + h = 15$

41. $\dfrac{s}{-4} = 9$

42. $-8c = 64$

43. $a - 13 = 4$

44. $e + 35 = -50$

Copyright © by Holt McDougal.
All rights reserved.

Holt McDougal Mathematics

Answer these questions to summarize the important concepts from Chapter 11 in your own words.

1. Explain why −8 and 8 have the same absolute value.

2. Explain how to graph the point (−7, 9).

3. Explain how to evaluate $x - (-7)$ for $x = -6$.

4. Explain the rules for multiplying integers.

5. Explain the rules for dividing integers.

6. Explain how to solve the equation $5 + x = 12$.

For more review of Chapter 11:

- Complete the Chapter 11 Study Guide and Review on pages 640–642 of your textbook.

- Complete the Ready to Go On quizzes on pages 612 and 636 of your textbook.

Copyright © by Holt McDougal.
All rights reserved.

Holt McDougal Mathematics

Introduction to Probability

Lesson Objectives

Estimate the likelihood of an event and write and compare probabilities

Vocabulary

probability (p. 652) _____

Additional Examples

Example 1

Write *impossible, unlikely, as likely as not, likely,* or *certain* to describe each event.

A. You roll an even number on a standard number cube.

B. The month of February has 28 days.

Example 2

A. Write the probability 75% as a decimal and as a fraction.

75% = ☐   Write as a decimal.

75% = ☐ = ☐   Write as a fraction in simplest form.

B. Write the probability 0.8 as a fraction and as a percent.

0.8 = ☐ = ☐   Write as a fraction in simplest form.

0.8 = ☐   Write as a percent.

C. Write the probability $\frac{7}{50}$ as a decimal and as a percent.

$\frac{7}{50}$ = ☐ ÷ ☐ = ☐   Write as a decimal.

$\frac{7}{50} = \frac{7 \times 2}{50 \times 2}$ = ☐ = ☐ %   Write as a percent.

Copyright © by Holt McDougal.
All rights reserved.

Holt McDougal Mathematics

Example 3

A. On a standard number cube, there is a 50% chance of rolling a multiple of 2 and a $33\frac{1}{3}$% chance of rolling a multiple of 3. Is it more likely to roll a multiple of 2 or a multiple of 3?

Compare: $33\frac{1}{3}$% ☐ 50%

It is more likely to roll a multiple of ☐ .

Check It Out!

1. Write *impossible, unlikely, as likely as not, likely,* or *certain* to describe each event.

    Sallie thinks of a number between 1 and 1,000. Ryan guesses the number Sallie is thinking of.

2. Write the probability 0.6 as a fraction and as a percent.

3. When you spin a certain spinner, there is a 35% chance that it will land on house, a 22% chance it will land on car, and a 43% chance that it will land on bicycle. Is it more likely to land on bicycle or house?

Copyright © by Holt McDougal.
All rights reserved.

Holt McDougal Mathematics

Experimental Probability

Lesson Objectives

Find the experimental probability of an event

Vocabulary

experiment (p. 656) _____

outcome (p. 656) _____

event (p. 656) _____

trial (p. 656) _____

experimental probability (p. 656) _____

_____

Additional Examples

Example 1

For each experiment, identify the outcome shown.

A. tossing two coins

outcome shown: [   ]

Example 2

For one month, Mr. Crowe recorded the time at which his train arrived. He organized his results in a frequency table.

Time	6:50–6:52	6:53–6:56	6:57–7:00
Frequency	7	8	5

A. Find the experimental probability of the train arriving between 6:57 and 7:00.

$$P(\text{between 6:57 and 7:00}) \approx \frac{\text{number of times the event occurs}}{\text{total number of trials}}$$

$$= \boxed{} = \boxed{}$$

Copyright © by Holt McDougal.
All rights reserved.

Holt McDougal Mathematics

Example 3

Erika tossed a cylinder 30 times and recorded whether it landed on one of its bases or on its side. Based on Erika's experiment, which way is the cylinder more likely to land?

Outcome	On a base	On its side
Frequency	卌 IIII	I 卌 卌 卌 卌 I

Find the experimental probability of each outcome.

$P(\text{base}) \approx \dfrac{\text{number of times the event occurs}}{\text{total number of trials}} = \dfrac{\boxed{}}{\boxed{}}$

$P(\text{side}) \approx \dfrac{\text{number of times the event occurs}}{\text{total number of trials}} = \dfrac{\boxed{}}{\boxed{}}$

$\dfrac{9}{30} \boxed{} \dfrac{21}{30}$ Compare the probabilities.

It is more likely that the cylinder will land on its [   ].

Check It Out!

1. For the experiment, identify the outcome shown.

Counting Methods and Sample Spaces

Lesson Objectives

Use counting methods to find all possible outcomes

Vocabulary

sample space (p. 662) _____

Additional Examples

Example 1 **PROBLEM SOLVING APPLICATION**

Matt wants to take a 3-day weekend trip to visit his grandparents. He can take either Friday or Monday off from work, and he can either fly, drive, take a train, or take a bus. How many options are available to Matt?

1. **Understand the Problem**

   List the important information.

   • There are [____] days he can take off work.   • There are [____] types of transportation.

2. **Make a Plan**

   You can draw a [_____] to find all the possible trip combinations.

3. **Solve**

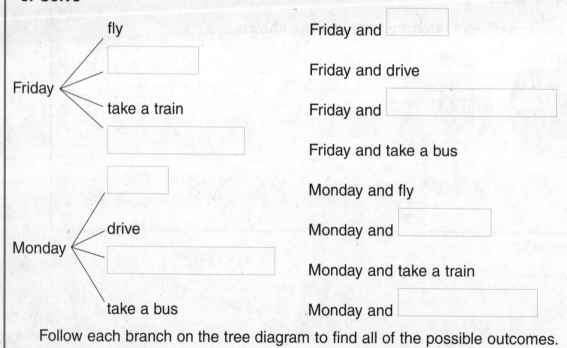

Follow each branch on the tree diagram to find all of the possible outcomes.

There are [____] different weekend trip combinations available to Matt.

Copyright © by Holt McDougal.
All rights reserved.

Holt McDougal Mathematics

4. Look Back

- There are ☐ branches at the end of the tree diagram. There are ☐ possible trip combinations.

Example 2

One girl and one boy will be chosen to go to the state science fair. The girl finalists are Alia, Brenda, Cathy, Deb, and Erika. The boy finalists are Frank, Greg, and Hal. How many different pairs of one girl and one boy can be formed?

- There are ☐ girls, A, B, C, D, and E.

- There are ☐ boys, F, G, and H.

Use each student's first initial.

- List all pairs that begin with A.   ☐

- List all pairs that begin with B.   ☐

- List all pairs that begin with C.   ☐

- List all pairs that begin with D.   ☐

- List all pairs that begin with E.   ☐

There are ☐ groups of ☐ pairs.

☐ + ☐ + ☐ + ☐ + ☐ = ☐

There are ☐ pairs of one girl and one boy.

Copyright © by Holt McDougal.
All rights reserved.

Holt McDougal Mathematics

Example 3

Rick wants to buy a mammal and a reptile for pets. The pet shop has dogs, cats, rabbits, hamsters, and ferrets, which are all mammals. It also has lizards, monitors, and boa constrictors, which are all reptiles. How many combinations of one mammal and one reptile are possible?

There are ☐ choices for mammals and ☐ choices for reptiles.

☐ · ☐ = ▭   Multiply the number of choices in each category.

There are ▭ possible combinations.

Check It Out!

1. For her work uniform, Missy has a choice of three colors of pants—black, khaki, or navy. She has four choices for shirt colors—red, white, green, and yellow. How many different uniforms can Missy wear?

2. One girl and one boy will be chosen to go to the movie preview. The girl finalists are Fay, Gerri, Heidi, and Ingrid. The boy finalists are Kevin, Larry, and Marc. How many different pairs of one girl and one boy can be formed?

3. Aubrey's Wing Shop offers three types of sauce: mild, medium, or hot. It also offers three flavors: original, garlic, or barbeque. How many combinations of one sauce and one flavor are possible?

Copyright © by Holt McDougal.
All rights reserved.

Holt McDougal Mathematics

Theoretical Probability

Lesson Objectives

Find the theoretical probability and complement of an event

Vocabulary

theoretical probability (p. 666) _____

_____

equally likely (p. 666) _____

_____

fair (p. 666) _____

_____

complement (p. 667) _____

_____

Additional Examples

Example 1

A. **What is the probability of this fair spinner landing on 3?**

There are [＿＿＿] possible outcomes when

spinning this spinner: 1, 2, or 3. All are [＿＿＿]

likely because the spinner is [＿＿＿].

$P(3) = \dfrac{\boxed{}}{3 \text{ possible outcomes}}$

There is only [＿＿＿] way for the spinner to land on 3.

$P(3) = \dfrac{1 \text{ way event can occur}}{3 \text{ possible outcomes}} = \boxed{}$

Copyright © by Holt McDougal.
All rights reserved.

Holt McDougal Mathematics

Example 2

Suppose there is a 45% chance of snow tomorrow. What is the probability that it will not snow?

In this situation there are two possible outcomes, either it will snow or it will not snow.

P(snow) + P(not snow) = ⬜ %

⬜ % + P(not snow) = ⬜ %

− 45%   − 45%   Subtract ⬜ % from each side.

P(not snow) = ⬜ %

Check It Out!

1. **What is the probability of rolling a number less than 4 on a fair number cube?**

2. **Suppose there is a 35% chance of rain tomorrow. What is the probability that it will not rain?**

Copyright © by Holt McDougal.
All rights reserved.

Holt McDougal Mathematics

Compound Events

Lesson Objectives

List all the outcomes and find the theoretical probability of a compound event

Vocabulary

compound event (p. 672) _____

_____

Additional Examples

Example 1

Jerome spins the spinner and rolls a fair number cube.

A. Find the probability of the number cube showing an even number and the spinner showing a B.

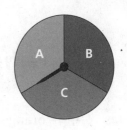

First find all of the possible outcomes.

Number Cube

Spinner		1	2	3	4	5	6
	A	1, A	2, A	3, A	4, A	5, A	6, A
	B	1, B	2, B	3, B	4, B	5, B	6, B
	C	1, C	2, C	3, C	4, C	5, C	6, C

There are [ ] possible outcomes, and all are equally likely.

[ ] of the outcomes have an even number and B: [ ] , [ ] ;

[ ] , [ ] ; and [ ] , [ ] .

$P(\text{even, B}) = \dfrac{3 \text{ ways events can occur}}{18 \text{ possible outcomes}}$

$= \dfrac{[\quad]}{[\quad]}$

$= [\quad]$ Write your answer in simplest form.

Copyright © by Holt McDougal.
All rights reserved.

Holt McDougal Mathematics

B. In the experiment on page 689, what is the probability of the coin showing tails, the spinner showing purple, and a green marble being chosen?

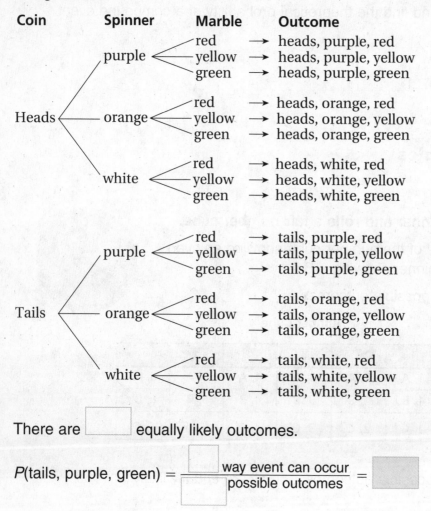

Coin	Spinner	Marble	Outcome
	purple	red	→ heads, purple, red
		yellow	→ heads, purple, yellow
		green	→ heads, purple, green
Heads	orange	red	→ heads, orange, red
		yellow	→ heads, orange, yellow
		green	→ heads, orange, green
	white	red	→ heads, white, red
		yellow	→ heads, white, yellow
		green	→ heads, white, green
	purple	red	→ tails, purple, red
		yellow	→ tails, purple, yellow
		green	→ tails, purple, green
Tails	orange	red	→ tails, orange, red
		yellow	→ tails, orange, yellow
		green	→ tails, orange, green
	white	red	→ tails, white, red
		yellow	→ tails, white, yellow
		green	→ tails, white, green

There are ⬚ equally likely outcomes.

$$P(\text{tails, purple, green}) = \frac{\boxed{}\ \text{way event can occur}}{\boxed{}\ \text{possible outcomes}} = \boxed{}$$

Check It Out!

1. Kiki spins the spinner and rolls a fair number cube.

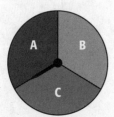

Find the probability of the number cube showing an odd number and the spinner showing A. ⬚

Copyright © by Holt McDougal.
All rights reserved.

Holt McDougal Mathematics

Making Predictions

Lesson Objectives

Use probability to predict events

Vocabulary

prediction (p. 680) _____

_____

population (p. 680) _____

_____

sample (p. 680) _____

_____

Additional Examples

Example 1

A. A store claims that 78% of shoppers end up buying something. Out of 1,000 shoppers, how many would you predict will buy something?

You can write a proportion. Remember that percent means "per hundred."

$$\frac{78}{100} = \frac{x}{1,000}$$ Think: ☐ out of 100 is how many out of

☐ ?

$$100 \cdot x = 78 \cdot 1,000$$ The cross products are ☐.

☐ x = ☐ x is multiplied by ☐.

$$\frac{100x}{100} = \frac{78,000}{100}$$ ☐ both sides by ☐ to

undo the ☐.

$$x = \boxed{}$$

You can predict that about ☐ out of 1,000 customers will buy

something.

Copyright © by Holt McDougal.
All rights reserved.

Holt McDougal Mathematics

Example 2

If you roll a number cube 30 times, how many times do you except to roll a number greater than 2?

$P(\text{greater than } 2) = \frac{4}{6} = \frac{2}{3}$

$\frac{2}{3} = \frac{x}{30}$ Think: 2 out of 3 is how many out of 30.

$3 \cdot x = 2 \cdot 30$ The cross products are [   ].

[   ]$x = 60$ x is multiplied by 3.

$\frac{3x}{3} = \frac{60}{3}$ [   ] both sides by [   ] to

undo the [   ].

$x =$ [   ]

You can expect to roll a number greater than 2 about [   ] times.

Example 3   PROBLEM SOLVING APPLICATION

A stadium sells yearly parking passes. If you have a parking pass, you can park at that stadium for any event during that year.

The managers of the stadium estimate that the probability that a person with a pass will attend any one event is 50%. The parking lot has 400 spaces. If the managers want the lot to be full at every event, how many passes should they sell?

1. Understand the Problem

The answer will be the number of parking passes they should sell. List the important information:

• $P(\text{person with pass attends event}): =$ [   ]%

• There are [   ] parking spaces.

Copyright © by Holt McDougal.
All rights reserved.

Holt McDougal Mathematics

2. Make a Plan

The managers want to fill all [ ] spaces. But on average, only

[ ] % of parking pass holders will attend. So 50% of the pass holders

must equal 400. You can write an equation to find this number.

3. Solve

$\dfrac{50}{100} = \dfrac{400}{x}$ Think: 50 out of [ ] is 400 out of how many?

$100 \cdot 400 = 50 \cdot x$ The cross products are [ ].

$40,000 = \boxed{} x$ x is multiplied by [ ].

$\dfrac{40,000}{50} = \dfrac{50x}{50}$ [ ] both sides by 50 to undo the

[ ].

$\boxed{} = x$

The managers should sell [ ] parking passes.

4. Look Back

If the managers sold only 400 passes, the parking lot would not usually be full because only about 50% of the people with passes will attend any one event. The managers should sell more than 400 passes, so 800 is a reasonable answer.

Check It Out!

1. A store claims 62% of shoppers end up buying something. Out of 1,000 shoppers, how many would you predict will buy something?

2. If you roll a number cube 90 times, how many times do you expect to roll a factor of 4?

Copyright © by Holt McDougal.
All rights reserved.

Holt McDougal Mathematics

12-1 Introduction to Probability

Write *impossible, unlikely, as likely as not, likely,* **or** *certain* **to describe each event.**

1. This week has 7 days.

2. The spinner lands on the color purple.

3. The spinner lands on white.

12-2 Experimental Probability

For each experiment, identify the outcome shown.

4. spinning a spinner

5. tossing two coins

Jake recorded the number of strikes he bowled in his last 20 games. He organized his results in a frequency table.

number of strikes	0	1	2	3	4
frequency	2	8	5	3	2

6. Find the experimental probability that Jake will get one strike in a game.

7. Based upon Jake's results, what are the two numbers of strikes he has an equal chance of getting?

12-3 Counting Methods and Sample Spaces

8. Shannon is shopping for a cell phone case. The cell phone cases come in black, white, red, blue, and pink. She can choose between cell phones with a car charger and cell phones without a car charger. What are the possible cell phone combinations Shannon can choose from?

9. Megan will choose a blouse, a shirt, and a pair of shoes from her closet to wear to school. Find the number of different outfits she can make if she has

    a. 3 blouses, 4 skirts, 2 pairs shoes

    b. 5 blouses, 2 skirts, 3 pairs shoes

12-4 Theoretical Probability

10. What is the probability of rolling a number that is a multiple of 2 on a fair number cube?

11. What is the probability of rolling a prime number on a fair number cube?

12. What is the probability of rolling either a 4 or a 5 on a fair number cube?

13. What is the probability of NOT rolling a 1 on a fair number cube?

14. Suppose there is a 60% chance of rain tomorrow. What is the probability it will NOT rain tomorrow?

15. Suppose there is a 79% chance of Lance making a free throw. What is the probability that Lance will NOT make a free throw?

Copyright © by Holt McDougal.
All rights reserved.

Holt McDougal Mathematics

12-5 Compound Events

16. Bob rolled a fair number cube twice. Find the probability that the number cube will show an even number on the first roll and an odd number on the second roll.

An experiment involves spinning each spinner once. Find each probability.

17. P(3 on the first spinner and 7 on the second spinner)

18. P(NOT a 3 on the first spinner and 8 on the second spinner)

19. P(NOT a 4 on the first spinner and NOT a 6 on the second spinner)

20. P(1 or 2 on the first spinner and NOT a 5 on the second spinner)

12-6 Making Predictions

21. Based on a sample survey, a broadcasting company claims that 78% of the household televisions were tuned into the new reality series on Tuesday night. Out of 40,000 households, how many would you predict watched the new reality series?

22. A sack holds 4 orange marbles, 2 green marbles, 3 red marbles, and 1 clear marble. You pick a marble from the sack, record its color, and place the marble back in the sack. If you repeat this process 50 times, how many times do you expect to pick a red marble from the sack?

Copyright © by Holt McDougal.
All rights reserved.

Holt McDougal Mathematics

Big Ideas

Answer these questions to summarize the important concepts from Chapter 12 in your own words.

1. Explain how to find the experimental probability of an event.

2. Explain how to use the Fundamental Counting Principle to find the total number of possible outcomes for an event.

3. Explain how to find the theoretical probability of rolling a number greater than 2 on a fair number cube.

4. Explain how to find the complement of an event.

5. Explain how to predict the number of times you can expect to roll a 3 when rolling a number cube 210 times.

For more review of Chapter 12:

• Complete the Chapter 12 Study Guide and Review on pages 688–690 of your textbook.

• Complete the Ready to Go On quizzes on pages 670 and 684 of your textbook.

Copyright © by Holt McDougal.
All rights reserved.

Holt McDougal Mathematics

Tables and Functions

Lesson Objectives

Use data in a table to write an equation for a function and use the equation to find a missing value

Vocabulary

function (p. 698) _____

_____

input (p. 698) _____

_____

output (p. 698) _____

_____

Additional Examples

Example 1

Write an equation for a function that gives the values in the table. Use the equation to find the value of *y* for the indicated value of *x*.

x	3	4	5	6	7	10
y	13	16	19	22	25	

y is ☐ times *x* + ☐.   Compare *x* and *y* to find a pattern.

y = ☐☐☐   Use the pattern to write an equation.

y = 3(☐) + 4   Substitute ☐ for *x*.

y = ☐ + ☐ = ☐   Use your function rule to find *y* when

$x =$ ☐

Copyright © by Holt McDougal.
All rights reserved.

Holt McDougal Mathematics

Example 2

Write an equation for the function. Tell what each variable you use represents.

The height of a painting is 7 times its width.

$h = $ [   ] of painting   Choose [   ] for the equation.

$w = $ [   ] of painting

[   ]   Write an equation.

Example 3 PROBLEM SOLVING APPLICATION

The school choir tracked the number of tickets sold and the total amount of money received. They sold each ticket for the same price. They received $80 for 20 tickets, $88 for 22 tickets, and $108 for 27 tickets. Write an equation for the function.

1. **Understand the Problem**

   The answer will be an equation that describes the relationship between the

   number of [   ] sold and the money [   ].

2. **Make a Plan**

   You can make a table to display the data.

3. **Solve**

   Let t be the number of [   ]. Let m be the amount of

   [   ] received.

t	20	22	27
m	80	88	108

   m is equal to [   ] times t.   Compare t and m.

   [   ]   Write an equation.

4. Look Back

Substitute the t and m values in the table to check that they are solutions of the equation $m = 4t$.

$m = 4t$ (20, 80) $m = 4t$ (22, 88) $m = 4t$ (27, 108)

$80 \overset{?}{=} 4 \cdot 20$ $88 \overset{?}{=} 4 \cdot 22$ $108 \overset{?}{=} 4 \cdot 27$

$80 \overset{?}{=} 80 \checkmark$ $88 \overset{?}{=} 88 \checkmark$ $108 \overset{?}{=} 108 \checkmark$

Check It Out!

Write an equation for a function that gives the values in the table. Use the equation to find the value of y for the indicated value of x.

1.

x	3	4	5	6	7	10
y	10	12	14	16	18	

2. Write an equation for the function. Tell what each variable you use represents.

The height of a mirror is 4 times its width.

3. The school choir tracked the number of tickets sold and the total amount of money received. They sold each ticket for the same price. They received $60 for 20 tickets, $66 for 22 tickets, and $81 for 27 tickets. Write an equation for the function.

Copyright © by Holt McDougal.
All rights reserved.

Holt McDougal Mathematics

Graphing Functions

Lesson Objectives

Represent linear functions using ordered pairs and graphs

Vocabulary

linear equation (p. 703) _____

_____

Additional Examples

Example 1

Use the given *x*-values to write solutions of the equation as ordered pairs.

$y = 4x + 2$; $x = 1, 2, 3$

Make a [   ] table by using the given values for *x* to find

values for *y*.

Write these solutions as [   ] pairs.

x	4x + 2	y		(x, y)
[ ]	[ ]	[ ]		[ ]
[ ]	[ ]	[ ]		[ ]
[ ]	[ ]	[ ]		[ ]

Example 2

Determine whether the ordered pair is a solution to the given equation.

(3, 21); $y = 7x$

$\quad\quad y = 7x$ Write the equation.

$\boxed{} \overset{?}{=} 7(\boxed{})$ Substitute $\boxed{}$ for *x* and 21 for $\boxed{}$.

$21 \overset{?}{=} 21 \checkmark$

So ([   ]) is a solution to $y = 7x$.

Copyright © by Holt McDougal.
All rights reserved.

Holt McDougal Mathematics

Example 3

Use the graph of the linear function to find the value of *y* for the given value of *x*.

x = 4

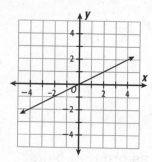

Start at the origin and move ☐ units ☐.

Move ☐ until you reach the graph. Move left to find the *y*-value on the ☐.

When *x* = 4, *y* = ☐. The ordered pair is (☐).

Example 4

Graph the function described by the equation.

$y = -x - 2$

Make a function table.

x	$-x - 2$	*y*
☐	☐	☐
☐	☐	☐
☐	☐	☐

Write these solutions as ordered pairs.

(x, y)

Graph the ☐ pairs on a ☐ plane.

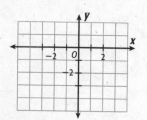

Draw a line through the points to represent ☐ the values of ☐ you could have chosen and the ☐ values of *y*.

Copyright © by Holt McDougal.
All rights reserved.

Holt McDougal Mathematics

LESSON 13-2 *CONTINUED*

Check It Out!

1. Use the given *x*-values to write solutions of the equation $y = 3x + 2$ as ordered pairs.

   $x = 2, 3, 4, 5.$

2. Determine whether the ordered pair is a solution to the given equation.

   $(4, 20); y = 5x$

3. Use the equation below to find the value of *y* for the given value of *x*.

   $y = 3x - 2$

   $x = 2.$

4. Graph the function described by the equation $y = -x - 4.$

Copyright © by Holt McDougal.
All rights reserved.

Holt McDougal Mathematics

Slope and Rate of Change

Lesson Objectives

Find rates of change and slopes

Vocabulary

rate of change (p. 706) _____

_____

slope (p. 707) _____

Additional Examples

Example 1

Tell whether the rates of change are constant or variable.

A.   +2   + ☐   + ☐   + ☐

x	2	4	7	8	10
y	5	11	20	23	29

                    +6   + ☐   + ☐   + ☐

Find the [   ] between consecutive data points.

Find each [   ] of the change in y to the change in x.

$\frac{2}{6} =$ ☐ $\frac{3}{9} =$ ☐ $\frac{1}{3}$ $\frac{2}{6} =$ ☐

The rates of change are [   ].

Copyright © by Holt McDougal.
All rights reserved.

Holt McDougal Mathematics

Example 2

The table shows the driving distances that Jesse recorded.

Time (min)	0	5	10	15	20
Time (miles)	0	3	6	9	12

A. Determine whether the rates of change are constant or variable.

[ ] $\dfrac{5}{3}$ [ ]   [ ]

The rates of change are [ ] .

B. Graph the data and connect the points with line segments. If the rate of change is constant, find and interpret the slope.

The rate of change between any two points is [ ] .

The slope of the line is [ ] .

The slope is [ ] . This means he drove [ ] for every [ ] .

Check It Out!

1. Determine whether the rates of change are constant or variable.

x	0	2	5	6	9
y	5	15	30	35	50

Solving Two-Step Equations

Lesson Objectives

Solve two-step equations

Additional Examples

Example 1

Solve each equation.

A. 18 + 3x = 30

$$18 + 3x = 30$$

$$\underline{-18} \qquad \underline{-18} \qquad$$ Subtract ☐ from both sides to undo the addition.

$$3x = \boxed{}$$

$$\frac{3x}{3} = \frac{12}{3}$$ Divide both sides by ☐ to undo the multiplication.

$$x = \boxed{}$$

Check 18 + 3x = 30

$$18 + 3(\boxed{}) \stackrel{?}{=} 30$$

$$18 + \boxed{} \stackrel{?}{=} 30$$

$$30 \stackrel{?}{=} 30 \checkmark$$

B. $\frac{x}{3} - 2 = 1$

$$\frac{x}{3} - 2 = 1$$

$$\boxed{} \quad \boxed{}$$ Add ☐ to both sides to undo the subtraction.

$$\frac{x}{3} = \boxed{}$$

$$3 \cdot \frac{x}{3} = 3 \cdot 3$$ Multiply both sides by ☐ to undo the multiplication.

$$x = \boxed{}$$

Copyright © by Holt McDougal.
All rights reserved.

Holt McDougal Mathematics

Example 2

Nancy saved $87 of the money she made babysitting. She wants to buy CDs that cost $15 each, along with a set of headphones that cost $12. How many CDs can she buy?

A. Write a two step-equation to represent the situation.

Let x represent the number of [ ] purchased.

cost of a CD times + cost of headphones = total amount earned
the number of CDs

[ ]   +   [ ]   =   [ ]

The equation [ ] represents the situation.

B. Solve the equation.

$$15x + 12 = 87$$

$$\underline{-12 \quad -12} \qquad \text{Subtract } [\ ] \text{ from both sides.}$$

$$15x = [\ ]$$

$$\frac{15x}{15} = \frac{75}{15} \qquad \text{Divide both sides by } [\ ] \text{ to undo the multiplication.}$$

$$x = [\ ]$$

Nancy can buy [ ] CDs.

Check It Out!

1. Solve $\dfrac{x-5}{2} = 4$.

2. Keke earned $425 last week. She wants to put $350 in the bank, and buy some DVDs. Each DVD costs $25. Write a two-step equation to represent the situation. Then solve the equation. How many DVDs can she buy?

Copyright © by Holt McDougal.
All rights reserved.

Holt McDougal Mathematics

Inequalities

Lesson Objectives

Solve one-step inequalities.

Vocabulary

inequality (p. 718) _____

_____

solution of an inequality (p. 718) _____

_____

Additional Examples

Example 1

Graph the solution of each inequality on a number line.

A. $t > -1$

Draw a(n) [____] circle at [____] to show that -1 is [____] solution.

Shade to the [____] to show that values [____] than -1 are solutions.

B. $y \le -2$

Draw a(n) [____] circle at [____] to show that -2 is [____] solution.

Shade to the [____] to show that values [____] than -2 are solutions.

Copyright © by Holt McDougal.
All rights reserved.

Holt McDougal Mathematics

Example 2

Solve and graph the inequality.

$x - 3 \geq 5$

$x - 3 \geq 5$ 3 is [   ] from y.

$\underline{+3 \quad +3}$ Add [   ] to each side of the inequality.

$x \geq$ [   ]

The [   ] circle at [   ] shows that [   ] is a solution.

0 1 2 3 4 5 6 7 8 9 10 11

Example 3

Solve and graph the inequality.

$8z < 32$

$8z < 32$ 8 is [   ] by z.

$\frac{8z}{8} <$ [   ]   Divide both sides of the inequality by [   ] to undo the division.

$z <$ [   ]

The [   ] circle at [   ] shows that [   ] is not a solution.

-2 0 2 4 6 8 10

Check It Out!

1. Graph the solution of the inequality on a number line.

$b \leq 4$

Copyright © by Holt McDougal.
All rights reserved.

Holt McDougal Mathematics

Solving Two-Step Inequalities

Lesson Objectives

Solve two-step inequalities.

Additional Examples

Example 1

Solve and graph each inequality.

A. $3y + 6 > 12$

$3y + 6 > 12$

$\underline{-6 \quad -6}$ Subtract ▢ from each side of the inequality to undo the addition.

$3y > 6$

$\dfrac{3y}{3} > $ ▢ Divide both sides of the inequality by ▢ to undo the multiplication.

$y > $ ▢

Place a(n) ▢ circle at ▢ , and then shade to the ▢ .

B. $\dfrac{t}{3} + 3 \geq 12$

$\dfrac{t}{3} + 3 \geq 12$

$\underline{-3 \quad -3}$ Subtract ▢ from each side of the inequality to undo the addition.

$\dfrac{t}{3} \geq 9$

$3 \cdot \dfrac{t}{3} \geq 3 \cdot 9$ Multiply both sides of the inequality by ▢ to undo the division.

$t \geq $ ▢

Place a(n) ▢ circle at ▢ , and then shade to the ▢ .

Copyright © by Holt McDougal.
All rights reserved.

Holt McDougal Mathematics

Example 2 **PROBLEM SOLVING APPLICATION**

The cost to rent a party room is $70. There is an additional fee of $8 per guest.
How many guests can Jesse invite if he can spend no more than $150?

1. **Understand the Problem**
   The answer will be the number of guests Jesse can invite.
   List the important information:
   • It costs $70 to rent a party room.
   • It costs $8 for each guest.
   • Jesse can spend no more than $150.

2. **Make a Plan**
   Write and solve an inequality. Let x equal the unknown number of guests. The
   amount of money spent must be less than or equal to $150.

   cost for one guest times + cost of party room   must be less   total cost
   the number of guests   than or equal

   [ ]   +   [ ]   ≤   [ ]

3. **Solve**
   $8x + 70 \le 150$ Write the inequality.

   $\underline{-70 \quad -70}$ Subtract from each side of the inequality to undo
                               the addition.

   $8x \le$ [ ]

   $\frac{8x}{8} \le$ [ ]   Divide both sides of the inequality by [ ] to undo the
                               multiplication.

   $x \le$ [ ]

   Jesse can invite no more than [ ] guests.

4. **Look Back**
   Substitute 10 into the original inequality to see if it holds true.

Check It Out!

1. Solve and graph the inequality.

   $2m - 3 < 7$

Copyright © by Holt McDougal.
All rights reserved.
Holt McDougal Mathematics

Chapter Review

13-1 Tables and Functions

Write an equation for a function that gives the values in each table. Use the equation to find the value of *y* for the indicated value of *x*.

1.

x	1	2	3	6	10
y	3	7	11	23	■

2.

x	35	20	10	0	−15
y	−7	−4	■	0	3

Write an equation for the function. Tell what each variable you use represents.

3. Ashlynn earned three times as much allowance as her sister, Danica.

13-2 Graphing Functions

Graph the function described by each equation.

4. $y = 3x + 1$

x	−1	0	1	2
y	■	■	■	■

5. $y = x - 4$

x	−1	0	1	2
y	■	■	■	■

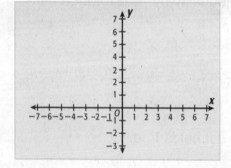

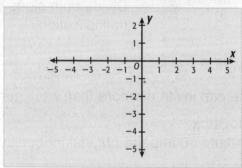

13-3 Slope and Rate of Change

Tell whether the rates of change are constant or variable.

6.

x	1	2	4	7	8
y	2	4	6	7	10

7.

x	0	2	5	7	10
y	3	9	18	24	33

Copyright © by Holt McDougal.
All rights reserved.

Holt McDougal Mathematics

13-4 Solving Two-Step Equations

Solve each equation.

8. $4x + 2 = 10$ **9.** $\frac{k}{3} + 1 = 4$ **10.** $5n - 8 = -3$ **11.** $\frac{d}{4} + 7 = 9$

12. $\frac{h}{6} + 7 = 13$ **13.** $9y + 4 = 7$ **14.** $8a - 12 = -6$ **15.** $\frac{t}{2} + 3 = 10$

13-5 Inequalities

Solve and graph each inequality.

16. $x - 3 > 1$ **17.** $\frac{m}{2} \le 4$

18. $6p \ge 42$ **19.** $z + 7 < 8$

13-6 Solving Two-Step Inequalities

20. Alexander's scores on the first four math exams were 82, 86, 92, and 96. What score can Alexander earn on the fifth exam to ensure an average of at least 91?

21. The cost of purchasing a car is $18,000. Jacob put a $10,000 down payment on the car. Each month he will make a payment of no more than $400. Disregarding interest, what is the greatest number of months it will take Jacob to pay for the car?

Copyright © by Holt McDougal.
All rights reserved.

Holt McDougal Mathematics

1. Explain how to determine if an ordered pair is a solution of an equation.

2. Explain how to determine if the rates of change in a table are constant or variable.

3. Explain how to solve the following two-step equation.

$\frac{x}{5} + 2 = 6$

4. Explain how to graph the following inequality.

$w > 2$

5. Explain how to check your answer to an inequality.

For more review of Chapter 13:

• Complete the Chapter 13 Study Guide and Review on pages 730–732 of your textbook.

• Complete the Ready to Go On quizzes on pages 712 and 726 of your textbook.

Copyright © by Holt McDougal.
All rights reserved.

Holt McDougal Mathematics